I Found All the Parts
Healing the Soul Through Rock 'n' Roll

Laura Faeth

Sound of Your Soul

an imprint of Wyatt-MacKenzie

I Found All the Parts
Healing the Soul Through Rock 'n' Roll
Laura Faeth

FIRST EDITION

ISBN: 978-1-932279-91-7

Library of Congress Control Number: 2008929544

www.SoundOfYourSoul.com

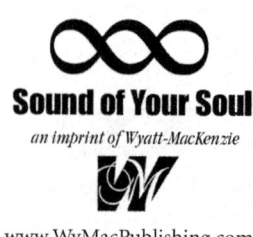

Sound of Your Soul
an imprint of Wyatt-MacKenzie

www.WyMacPublishing.com

Praise for *I Found All the Parts*

"Laura Faeth's ballsy, unrelenting faith in the power of music to shake the soul awake is a glorious reminder that all great art, especially the raunchy immediacy of rock 'n' roll, can lift you, dancing and spinning, into the holy stratosphere of the Now."
—Pamela Des Barres, author, *I'm with the Band*

"This book is fresh, original, raw, and expansive. Laura Faeth writes with honesty, spunk, and courage about unusual experiences that challenge our old thoughts about the nature of reality. I love and applaud her courage, honesty, and voice. This is one wild spiritual journey with an audacious guide."
—Tama J. Kieves, bestselling author, *This Time I Dance! Creating the Work You Love (How One Harvard Lawyer Left It All to Have It All!)*, www.ThisTimeIDance.com

"The journey towards self-love is a profound process that spans a lifetime. Laura's mystical experiences incorporate sound principles for spiritual awakening and self-actualization, set to the beat of our modern times. I thoroughly enjoyed her heartfelt commitment to soulful transcendence, and her willingness to share this with the world."
—Joy Rose, President and Founder, Mamapalooza

"Laura Faeth has given us a tome; an *Eat, Pray, Love* meets *Almost Famous* melding of the mystical and the musical that courageously asks the question, 'Can we really heal the soul through rock 'n' roll?' The answer is a Marshall Stack 'this one goes to *11*' yes!"
—Lonn Friend, author, *Life on Planet Rock*

"Get ready for the ride of your life! *I Found All the Parts* is a mind expanding trip through cutting edge metaphysics via fervent music fandom. Laura is an alchemist, turning her experiences following a band into a humorous yet enlightening story filled with profound knowledge and inspired insight. If you're a musician, a music lover, or just someone who knows that there is a deeper reality out there, then crack open this book, strap yourself in, and prepare for a consciousness-altering joyride like you've never experienced. This book did nothing less than completely transform my creative path, my spiritual journey, and the way I view the world. It can happen for you too!"

—Pam Moore, musician: The Neptunas, Cheap Chick, and Madame Pamita

"Laura Faeth's fascinating explorations and revelations about our attraction to particular music and rock bands successfully—and humorously—help spur us into our own personal journey towards awareness and personal empowerment. A must-read to discover more about the soul, multidimensional lives and relationships, and what we resonate to (and why) in rock music."

—E. Nora H. Amrani, Ch.T., author, Consciousness Consultant, and healer, www.vibrani.com

"*I Found All the Parts* offers the reader a bird's eye view on how intuitive, spiritual guidance can place signposts under our nose to provide a deeper and more profound awareness of who we truly are. Laura Faeth has created an amazing tapestry of esoteric teachings as she melds metaphysical concepts to assist your understanding of who you truly are at the soul level. Whether you believe that you are a soul currently living a physical existence or not, you'll find this new book a fun and stimulating read that can take you places in your own personal examination that you have never considered."

—Dr. Linda R. Backman, licensed psychologist, author, *Bringing Your Soul to Light: Healing through Past Lives and the Time Between*, www.RavenHeartCenter.com

"In her maiden voyage, *I Found All the Parts: Healing the Soul through Rock 'n' Roll*, Laura Faeth has assembled spiritual, melodic, and literary elements to show we are all family. Reminiscent of a 1976 conversation with Jerry Garcia and Carlos Santana, Garcia explained to me about The Grateful Dead:

'Our relationship is part of the family concept. We're involved with a large number of people who know each other and it stays that way whether we work or not. I think almost all the people I've known around this area, involved around the music scene, have been faithful to that thing [the family concept].' Laura Faeth has indeed been faithful in her effort, and along the way delivered remedy with her sentiments, experiences, and ideas.

Santana suggested, 'To me, the real practicality is that some people are chosen instruments to carve a certain message, a certain mood.' Ms. Faeth has accomplished this task as well."

—Harvey Kubernik, author, *This is Rebel Music: The Harvey Kubernik Innerviews*

"Have *Faeth* in the process! *The Magical Mystery Tour* of life is *real* and is brought to the surface in this fascinating glimpse into one person's determination to put the pieces together from the universal river of flow."

—M. Joyce McMenamin, author, *The Integrity Channel* and editor of *NoNiche* and *Network Abundance* magazines

"You may never look at music the same way again. Not just for the spiritually inclined, Laura Faeth's remarkable book tickles, delights, and resonates from beginning to end. My sparkly hat is off to her! (Now who the bleep is TBIF?)"
    —Paula Berinstein, The Writing Show,
        www.writingshow.com

"Transcendent musical experiences—every music lover has had them, and any kind of music, from classical to jazz and rock, inspires them: ecstatic moments of feeling more alive, closer to the soul. Such events give permission and show the way to a higher level of self-integration, as this rollicking memoir of mystical experiences inspired by a famous rock band demonstrates. The book can be read as a guide to the new age for hard rockers or a guide to hard rock for new agers. Either way, it inspires a whole new view of the possibilities of music to heal."
    —Kurt Leland, author, *Music and the Soul: A Listener's
        Guide to Achieving Transcendent Musical Experiences*

"*I Found All the Parts* is so funny that I started laughing my tail off from the minute I picked it up. This is one book everyone should read."
    —Barbara Fara, editor, Musicincider.com

ACKNOWLEDGMENTS

Though writing a book is often a solitary process, without the support of the women in my Abraham group—Lisa Gillespie, Laura DeCurnou, Vicki McPherson, Leslie Hall, Anne Jurgensen, Galina Gilbert, Deb Openlander, Rochelle Schwartz, Marisa Haedike, and many others who visited our circle over time—this book wouldn't exist. They are all candidates for sainthood after listening to me drone on year after year about how everything in life intertwines with music, the Law of Attraction, and rock bands. I've asked the Big Cheese to give each of them a halo, a free "get into heaven" pass, and a lifetime supply of earplugs.

I must thank the numerous intuitives who have guided me along my rock 'n' roll spiritual path: Jalynn Venis, Carolyn Eberle, Jan Main, Dr. Caron Goode, Lee Cook, Rebecca Border, Heidi Petersen Ph.D., Charol Messenger, Diana, Danae Shanti, and the students at Psychic Horizons. Your profound insights added integral pieces to this complex reincarnation puzzle. Without you, I never would have mustered the confidence to trust my own intuition. My intuitive campadre Anne Jurgensen gets a special shout-out. I wouldn't be writing this acknowledgment if not for your wisdom, friendship, and love.

Many people claim that writing a book is incredibly difficult. Ha! Translating my transcendent concepts from their initial disemboweled hideous hagfish state to prose that read intelligently, was a gazillion times more challenging. Thanks to my publisher Nancy Cleary at Wyatt-MacKenzie and my editors Michelle Cook, Charol Messenger, Stephanie Gunning, Frank Boros, and Jenny Knuth, my book reads real pretty. The snazzy cover was designed by the incredibly talented (and handsome) Rich Gorey. He also created the amazing book trailer videos for *I Found All the Parts*, which can be viewed on my website soundofyoursoul.com.

Special thanks to fellow writer and keen-sighted editor, Lisa Gillespie. Your willingness to read and comment on numerous drafts of my book—the first was a 600-page single paragraph (it took me awhile to grasp the concept of chapters)—deserves special merit. Only a close soul companion would go to such great lengths. Thanks for being my sounding board and a great friend.

Thank you music fan Sundante. You are a brave soul to traverse this bizarre rock 'n' roll odyssey with me. I am incredibly grateful that the Law of Attraction drew us together. Finding you gave reassurance that at least one other fan on this planet recognized something deeper was taking place with our band's music.

Within days of asking for sound legal advice, angels sent attorney Kevin Houchin my way. Amazingly, he's not only a spiritual non-judgmental kind of guy, but a brilliant holistic lawyer and a Freemason. To have effortlessly found such a unique combination of attributes in my legal counsel confirmed yet once again that the Law of Attraction is real.

The Internet gets kudos for making the outrageous amount of research I needed easily accessible. Thanks to the countless folks whose websites provided obscure, esoteric insights that helped me piece together my hypothesis. Though the world may be going digital, some of us old farts still love those passé relics called books. To the numerous authors whose texts I scoured: you rock.

There are so many others to acknowledge, I can't possibly name everyone. But I must thank my mom, husband, and two daughters who kept me grounded throughout this unfolding. I am so glad our souls chose to be family in this lifetime.

And last but not least, thanks to the rock band I followed and their fans. My soul deeply appreciates your joining me on my awakening journey. Our passion for music is fueling a revolution in consciousness. Are we finally hearing the call to

WAKE THE BLEEP UP!?

I Found All the Parts

TABLE OF CONTENTS

PART THREE

PART FOUR

FOREWORD
SING-CHRONICITY

I was in Iron Maiden's hospitality hang, post their L.A. Forum performance last winter, chatting it up with guests and friends of the iconic British band. After Metallica drummer Lars Ulrich—who authored the foreword to *my* memoir, *Life on Planet Rock*, made sure I was 'doing okay, man,' I drifted over to engage Metallica bassist Robert Trujillo. Within sixty seconds we were discussing the cosmos, astrology, and numerology, specifically, the number 11.

"Dude, you see 'em, too?" he smiled widely. "I've been getting into this whole 11:11 thing. The gateway. Are you hip to that stuff? It's wild!" The bass-ass banger of the four-string I'd known since his Suicidal Tendencies days had found a kindred spirit. While the rest of the room discussed professional machinations through the prism of 100-proof old-school decadence, two pilgrims on a similar path pondered the infinite. "I see 11s every day, dude," I responded. "We're blessed. Those who see 11s have reached a unique level of consciousness. My Kundalini yogi Guru Singh says the two 'ones' reflect one another, putting you on equal footing with the divine."

Slayer's Kerry King—lead guitarist for trash metal's most devilish heroes who released their LP, *God Hates Us All*, on September 11, 2001—entered the frame to say hello and celestial conversation gave way to two veteran warriors of rock doing their 'bro' thing as I drifted off, enamored by the dark/light synchronicity of the moment.

Which brings us to the here, now, and 'wow' of this moment where a writer named Friend lends a few introductory words to an angel named Faeth. Over the past several months, since the Universe brought us together, that is what Laura Faeth has become to me. An angel. Reading *I Found All the Parts* was nothing short of a mystical experience. Page after page, epigram after epigram, revelation after revelation, synchronicity after synchronicity, I saw myself, and in that reflection, meditated on the lessons. Her personal narrative—self-realization and soul healing through a lifelong obsession with an 'anonymous' rock group (yes, I have known the mysterious minstrels for almost 20 years)—transcends an original, quirky, and fun read. Laura Faeth has given us a tome; an *Eat, Pray, Love* meets *Almost Famous* melding of the mystical and the musical that courageously asks the question, "Can we really heal the soul through rock 'n' roll?" The answer is a Marshall Stack 'this one goes to *11*' yes!

I'm not a critic. Never have been. It pains me to sit in judgment of another artist's work. Only those who choose to skate this slippery slope of expression know from whence their creativity comes. I possess an almost pathological empathy for the brave ones that can't sit by and let the world decompose without composing themselves. I'm in my 11th year of 'the shift.' Yes, that number again. It has become ubiquitous to my being since I was so lovingly bitch-slapped by the Universe in the spring of 1998 after four Faustian years as the highly paid, creatively strangled VP of A&R for Clive Davis' now defunct Arista Records. My first career failure and life pause sent me inward. Everything fell apart; my marriage, my life. I exiled myself to the desert, wrote my book, returned to L.A. in the spring of '06 and a day does not go by where I do not both condemn and bless the struggle. I am afloat on a river of constant change. Just like my angel, Laura Faeth.

"Friends are all souls that we've known in other lives. We're drawn to each other. Even if I have only known them a day, it doesn't matter. I'm not going to wait 'till I have known them for two years, because anyway, we must have met somewhere before, you know."
—George Harrison

This epigram introducing part two of *I Found All the Parts* synthesizes the synchronicity for why I'm here on these pages. In my memoir, I open the chapter titled, "Chicken Soup for the Rubber Soul," with the sentence, "I emerged from my mother's womb on July 29, 1956, but I was born on February 9, 1964, the day the Beatles first performed on the Ed Sullivan show." The Fab Four sparked my musical consciousness. George Harrison shares the same birthday with my friend, veteran scribe, Harvey Kubernik, who read Laura's book yesterday and offered a quote for the sleeve. As for the numbers: 29th, two and nine = 11. '56, five and six = 11. Feb 9th, two and nine = 11.

This book hits stores on 11/11/08. Beyond the numbers, the words, and the riffs, get into the meditation. Sit cross-legged on the floor for a moment, close your eyes, and simply behold the wonder of what can happen when you do, indeed, finally find all the parts. Then open your mouth and SING.

I know I will.

Lonn Friend
September 11, 2008
Hollywood, California

INTRODUCTION

"BEGINNINGS"

—Chicago

"Music is spiritual and is a doorway into that world. Its power comes from the fact that it plugs directly into the soul, unlike a lot of visual art or text information that has to go through the more filtering processes of the brain."[1]

—Peter Gabriel, musician

This book bridges two seemingly different worlds: spirituality and rock 'n' roll.

My curiosity about the mystical emerged in early childhood. My attraction to rock music blossomed as a teenager. Yet as an adult, I never believed that my two passions had anything in common…until one cold January night in 2002 when my life changed forever. I had been living a typical, ho-hum life, married with two young kids, when a classic rock band triggered within me a transforming spiritual awakening. The odyssey I traversed with this rock band is the essence of this book.

This voyage has given me greater self-confidence, a sense of purpose, and taught me to pay attention, trust my intuition, and **Wake the Bleep Up!** Perhaps most surprising, I now know that I am never alone and time is an illusion. All of this thanks to a classic rock band and their music.

Out of respect for the members of the band I follow, I do not mention their names or the name of their band. Nor have I personally met any of the guys who spurred me on this journey. My spiritual awakening occurred solely through listening to their music and attending their concerts.

Since my journey led me to numerous spiritual and musical concepts, key words and phrases are highlighted in bold and defined in an online glossary with links at the website www.soundofyoursoul.com. Images of Tarot cards discussed in the book are located in the appendix.

Many concepts explored in the following pages, such as the Law of Attraction, are becoming more well-known due to popular movies such as *What the Bleep Do We Know?* and *The Secret.* Since 1995, long before these films were a twinkle in their producers' eyes, I had been studying and questioning the Law of Attraction. The idea that people who think alike, or carry a similar energy, are drawn together via this Law made me repeatedly challenge my long-time attraction to this well-known rock band and their music. *What's a spiritual, goody-two-shoes girl like me doin' in a place like this?* I wondered. *A rock concert?* Seemed more like opposites attracting. But, I eventually discovered that things aren't always as they seem.

Aldous Huxley wrote in his book *The Doors of Perception,* "When the doors of perception are cleansed, we will see things as they really are—infinite."[2] Jim Morrison named his group The Doors after this book and his signature song, "Break on Through," described his group's mystical mission: "There are things that are known, and things that are unknown, and in-between are the Doors."[3]

I invite you to walk through your own doors of perception and join me as I spiritually wake up and enter a world of archetypes, myths, intuition, reincarnation, and healing the soul with rock 'n' roll.

PART ONE

"Wake Up Little Susie"
—The Everly Brothers

On Waking Up

"Spirituality means waking up. Most people, even though they don't know it, are asleep. They're born asleep, they live asleep, they marry in their sleep, they breed children in their sleep, they die in their sleep without ever waking up. They never understand the loveliness and the beauty of this thing that we call human existence.... Waking up is unpleasant, you know. You are nice and comfortable in bed. It is irritating to be woken up."[4]

—Anthony de Mello, Jesuit priest

CHAPTER 1
"FAN MAIL"
—Blondie

"The rest of the band will follow me down any dark alley. Sometimes there's a light at the end of the alley, and sometimes there's a black hole. The point is, you don't get an adventure in music unless you're willing to take chances."
—Jerry Garcia, musician

Teenage girls just wanna have fun. For *this* girl, having a blast in the late 1970s on Long Island, NY, included going to Friday-night teen discos at the Knights of Columbus and confiding to my spandex-clad girlfriends which cute boy was my latest crush. If I wasn't doing the Hustle, you could find me in the basement, playing "Freebird" on my electric guitar with the neighborhood guys. Mom always knew when we had jammed downstairs, because the ear-splitting vibrations made the decorative plates in her china closet dance out of place. She would walk around the house bellowing, "Goddammit! Who moved my china again?"

My love of music went *waaay* back to the days of my rhythmic kicking in Mom's womb, keeping her awake all night. Even as a fetus, I could hear her yelling, "Goddammit, what are you doing in there? The Locomotion?"

On a hot summer's day in 1963, I'd had enough of being all cramped up, and I kicked my way to freedom out of my heavily sedated, unconscious mother's birth canal. But music would make the birth ordeal worthwhile.

The first time I saw a piano at age three, Dad had to use a

crowbar to pry me away from it. Fortunately, four years later, my neighbor bought a used upright and started giving me piano lessons. That was the happiest day of my young life.

Playing music was like discovering a psychotropic drug, and my parents encouraged me to be a user. Studying classical music over the next few years opened up a world of harmony and an appreciation for the brilliance of the great Masters. But it was during my high-school days that *contemporary* music became my melodic drug of choice, and I succumbed to being a total rock 'n' roll junkie. Chopin? Mozart? Beethoven? Roll over dead, guys. There're new kids in town—and they go by winsome names such as The Clash, AC/DC, The Cars, Foreigner, and Aerosmith.

My teenage daydreams often landed me at Madison Square Garden, playing in a rock band to thousands of screaming fans. I wasn't interested in being in an all-girl band like The Runaways. I *really* wanted to have fun. I longed to be a rock goddess, to play better than Clapton and be surrounded by boys who envied my prodigious talent.

But reality bites big time.

My plan to be a rock star was very short-lived. At age fifteen, I realized that, while my $65 black Les Paul copy edition Univox electric guitar (with humbucking pick-ups and holographic stickered-on pinstripes) looked spectacular, it could not overcome my god-awful playing. Despite the years of piano lessons, there wasn't a molecule of musical talent in my DNA.

So my guitar was coveted by many a teenage boy who secretly hoped I would take up the glockenspiel, each wanting to inherit my awesome "black baby." During a particularly loud pathetic jam session when Mom's plates danced a mile off their mark in the china closet, one of my partners-in-noise told me about a band his older brother was "totally into."

"Do they have a guitar as fine as mine?" I inquired.

"No. They have even better guitars than yours, Laura. In fact, the lead guitarist has, like, a couple of hundred guitars!"

"No way. It can't be true," I snottily replied. My nose stuck so high up in the air that I could snort a cirrus cloud.

But one day, he brought me their first three albums and dared me to listen. I hate it when dudes dare or double-dare ya, so I finally caved and put the most recent album on my turntable.

"Whoop de friggin' do. What's all the fuss about?" I quipped. "For a guy with hundreds of guitars, I'm so not impressed." My nose was hovering at high altitude.

But as a few more songs caught my ear, some of the tunes weren't that bad, so I decided to play their first album. After several spins, **WHAM!**, a rapid succession of metaphoric two-by-fours walloped me between the eyes—accompanied by a voice inside my head, yelling, **Wake the Bleep Up, Laura!** *This is the music you've been waiting for. This is it.* One moment, I was a normal deluded girl who thought she could be a rock star. Then, in the flash of my Kodak instamatic camera, I transformed into a die-hard rock fan.

When I finally took the time to look at the album covers, the lead singer—with his long Goldilocks hair—blew me away. There was a dramatic moment of recognition…as if I'd somehow *known* him before. He seemed so damn familiar, and reminded me of the Norse god Thor I'd seen in comic books. But it was the sultry resonance of his voice that drew me into a hypnotic whirlpool of teenage fantasy. Every guy in the band was cool—but not *too* cool. They weren't untouchable superstars like the Stones or Led Zeppelin. I could relate to *this* band (hereafter referred to as TBIF or The Band I Follow.)

I was officially hooked on their sound. My snooty highbrow nose was now sniveling in the dirt. This band's obvious genius for music threw my woeful lack of musical talent into sharp relief. Even the lead guitarist simply breathing onto his six strings created a far superior sound than the dreck that had been coming out of my shiny black baby. He played about a gazillion times better than me. One-eyed, deaf amputees played better than me.

With dreams of rock stardom dashed, I consoled myself by playing in the high-school band, and took up the French horn (no glockenspiels were available at school), much to my mother's chagrin.

"Why can't you play something nice and soft?" she asked, "Something that won't move my dishes? Like the flute?"

It killed my mom that her only child, anatomically a girl, dressed like a disheveled lumberjack and liked loud, unfeminine musical instruments.

Many bands and artists had graced my turntable, but my feeling toward TBIF was vastly different. The heavier the song, the harder I fell. Something about the bassist's intoxicating riffs on his Hamer 12-string bass lured me like a hypnotized cobra listening to a snake charmer's flute. I couldn't get enough of those deep, pounding vibrations in my body and, without comprehending why, their music touched my soul like nothing else I had ever heard.

For a long time, I had hoped to connect with others who shared my passion, but I knew less than a handful of fellow TBIF fans. I tried to turn the other kids onto TBIF, but no one was interested. Finally, a live album was released in the United States, and TBIF zoomed up the charts. Yay! Everyone now loved my band. But seemingly within nanoseconds, TBIF's popularity waned. By the time college rolled around, me, myself, and I were the only beings in my circle of friends who liked TBIF.

For nearly twenty years, I remained a fan and watched TBIF perform from afar—until 1997. I'd heard you could buy pricey VIP tickets for the first and second rows and I imagined what fun it would be to have a seat so close to the stage. In the past, I always ended up in row ZZZ and needed the Six Million Dollar Man's funky telescopic eyeball to zoom in on those little dots that were supposed to be rock stars.

By the time I checked into tickets, however, there weren't any seats available closer than the far right side of the thirteenth row. I'd been to at least a dozen TBIF concerts over the years and going to another show with crummy seats seemed pointless. My enthusiastic fandom had tapered off a tad over the decades—but a little voice inside urged me to buy a ticket anyway.

My arrival at the concert was, as some fans refer to it, "stupid early." There was hardly anyone in the theater except for me and a completely inebriated dude. As luck would have it, his seat was one over from mine. He kept trying to talk to me throughout the warm-up band's set, but his sluuuuuured speeeeeech rendered conversation pointless.

After the warm-up band ended, the dude stumbled back over to the bar. A female security guard got my attention and asked, "Was that guy bothering you?"

"He's a bit annoying, but harmless," I told her.

"Follow me," she said.

Before I realized what was happening, I was escorted to a seat in the *second* row, right in front of the lead guitarist! Something magical took place during the concert, like a light had turned from 100 to 100,000 watts of power. The smile on my face stretched all the way to Toledo. I was totally hooked on TBIF again.

At the time, getting closer to TBIF had seemed like dumb luck. But now I know it was most certainly fate. This concert was essential for my spiritual awakening. An inner voice grew louder and louder:

"WAKE THE BLEEP UP!"

One warm day in June 1998, TBIF performed at an outdoor music festival. As I stood in the crowd, waiting for them to come on stage, the names of the guys in the band did a foxtrot in my head.

Huh. That's weird.

Then their first names transformed into their four initials over and over. *It's just a silly acronym,* I contemplated to myself. *I must be doing too many crossword puzzles. Fuhgetaboutit.*

I tried to forget, but the initials, which sounded like the name Robert, kept popping into my noggin' out of the blue.

Intuition is a funny thing. Sometimes it hits us like a two-by-four; other times it appears like a breadcrumb trail. This "Robert" nudge, I realized later, was a really significant bread-crumb. I just didn't know it yet.

Several weeks after this strange repetition of TBIF's initials had inserted its way into my consciousness, I walked toward a picture of the band on the wall of my office at work. Nothing fancy. Just their 1997 Christmas postcard for fan-club members. (Don't laugh, I wear my Superfan-club badge with great pride!)

With colossal intensity, I looked straight at the photo and shouted inside my head, *Why am I so freakin' obsessed with you and your music?!*

A thought rang loud and clear back into my mind: *Because you've been together before.*

Together before??? NO WAY. NO BLEEPING WAY!

But after a moment of knee-jerk disbelief, I thought, *So, that's why I can't get these guys out of my head?* Suddenly, it all clicked into place and made complete sense. I'd had a past life with TBIF.

After my initial whack in the head about being with the band in a previous lifetime, my curiosity was definitely piqued. Every day, I looked at the picture of them in my office. *Nah. No way!! Past life with the band? What fantasy! Get a grip, girlfriend!*

But the idea gnawed at me. Several weeks later, my friend Lisa was holding a one-day workshop with two other healers, one of whom was a **channeller (intuitive).**

I considered taking the course and sheepishly asked if she thought it would be *loco* to ask the intuitive about a possible past life with the band. Lisa knew of my passion for their music. "Hey, if it's something important to you in your life, why not ask?"

At the workshop, I queried Jalynn, the channeller, whether or not I'd had a past life with any member of the band. (Most intuitives I've met listen to whale and dolphin song, not hard-rock music; not surprisingly, Jalynn was clueless about TBIF.)

"For twenty years," I said, "I've been a fan of a well-known rock band. In the past few weeks, an overwhelming feeling that we might have been together before has surfaced. Do you see anything?"

"Is this a hard rock kind of band?" she asked.

"Yes."

"The band seems amazed at their success and longevity. I see a warrior caste they used to be part of, that is in the process of reuniting a lot of the souls that followed them into battle. They do this through their music. Their music has a certain beat, a drum sound that beckons you. It creates a compulsion to be where they are. It's as if you can't resist."

"When I was sixteen," I said jokingly, "my attraction made sense. But what's up with this twenty years later? Why do I still love their music and get absolutely absorbed by it?"

"Because they are issuing a calling card, and you simply can't refuse this party."

I laughed. "Are we supposed to go to battle, or what?"

"It feels to me that it is an energetic gathering of souls in preparation for something that is coming up. Probably not in this lifetime. Possibly in a parallel lifetime or another dimension. Their music is a way of uniting the warriors of their old clan. This doesn't even feel like earth to me. This feels like another planet. Have you ever recalled past lives where you felt like you were a warrior?"

My jaw dropped. I recalled a very vivid dream where I was a soldier on a desolate planet, and there was going to be a war. The fear of war, especially nuclear war, has terrorized me since childhood. Growing up, I was pretty certain the human race would face mass annihilation. I never understood my fear of death at such a young age.

"That's why their music appeals to you," Jalynn said. "You've fought side by side with them. You are very bonded. This is a tribe or clan. The lead singer seems very charismatic. I'm getting the feeling of raw power, and the fans can't get enough of it."

After the reading, Jalynn commented that she didn't recall much of what she had visualized except that the environment was very unusual and had an orange sky. Of course I was wary. This couldn't possibly be real.

Then again, when first looking at TBIF's album covers, I had been amazed at how much the singer resembled the mythic Norse warrior god Thor (in my twisted teenage mind). Perhaps this was some kind of metaphorical imagery, since the superhero **Thor**'s comic books were stashed underneath my bed? Hmm…

Thor is often referred to as a protector of both the gods and humans against the forces of evil. Had the singer and band traded in their magical hammer for guitars and drums? Were loud musical instruments the new and improved way to protect humans against the forces of evil? At the time, the thought never even occurred to me.

Several months later, toward the end of 1998, I began voice lessons with Danae, a singer who also channels guidance. We hooked up weekly to aurally connect with the fetus growing within my womb. People had told me that babies like hearing their mother's voice, so I figured my unborn daughter would enjoy my singing in utero. (Despite our sonic bonding, years later when practicing my "do-re-mi's" in the car, she would yell, "Mommy, PLEASE sing solo...*So low* that I can't hear you." I can't blame the kid. When I belt out a rock tune, the sound is reminiscent of a dying wildebeest.)

I asked Danae if we could do a reading about my baby and also ask some questions regarding the band. "Danae, why am I so attracted to this band and their music? Why am I now getting strong feelings, after all these years, that we've been together before in another lifetime?"

"Many soul groups have incarnated during this generation, who have an encoded wake-up switch. As the year 2000 approaches, certain soul groups have set that etheric clock to heighten the vibration, so the millennial shift will be an enlightened state as much as possible. It is the vibration that speaks to you. It happens to be in the form of music. The pole for that energy is the lead singer."

Danae relayed a bunch of other esoteric information about human energy and the dynamics of sound. My head really hurt after the reading.

She also said that when people go to a concert, there is an encoded connection to the music, like a calling card, bringing us together. The wake-up switch she referred to was precisely how it had felt to me all these years with the **Wake the Bleep Up!** rant inside my mind.

Danae mentioned the year 2000. This grabbed my attention, because starting about 1985, TBIF began goofing around with counting down to the year 2000 on their merchandise. I, too, had been enamored with the year 2000. Even as a kid, I sensed something important would happen after the millennium. I never dreamed that in 2002, I'd begin writing this book.

I'd asked Danae if TBIF had played music in one of my past lives, and if that's why their sound zinged through my soul. Instead of a simple answer, I got a crash course in physics and human energy. Life with intuitives is mind-bending, to say the least.

Life with intuitives. That sounds so bizarre, because most people think it is all hogwash. My father didn't believe we have a sixth sense. That unseen world did not exist for him. Though he died when I was sixteen, I'm sure a part of him knows I'm writing a book about rock music and metaphysics. He's probably banging his head against a wall in heaven, moaning, "Ugh. Where did I go wrong? How can she believe this nonsense?" My folks were very nice people, but they weren't religious or into any woo-woo stuff. As a kid, I attended church alone for years.

Despite my parents' non-interest in God and new-agey subjects, my compulsive urge to explore the true nature of reality has always been overwhelming. Dipping my toes, hands, and big head into the fascinating world of the metaphysical kept nudging me to trust my own intuition. Over time, the nudges became really loud, and wouldn't shut the bleep up.

CHAPTER 2

"RULES OF ATTRACTION"

—Bananarama

"That certain feeling happened to me in a big way quite often with the first King Crimson. Amazing things would happen—I mean, telepathy, qualities of energy, things that I had never experienced before with music…you can't tell whether the music is playing the musician or the musician is playing the music."[5]   —Robert Fripp, musician

Ever since I was a kid, I have experienced all kinds of strange encounters with people who claim to have seen, felt, or heard the paranormal. Some even make *me* look normal.

My Girl Scout leader saw an alien spacecraft over her house, while watering her geraniums (not cannabis). A friend's mom had talked to her dead grandmother and received a favorite chicken-soup recipe from beyond. Various co-workers over the years have told me how they've seen ghosts and angels, had premonitions, and dreamed of future disasters. One woman had worked in a yogurt shop where a **discarnate** would goof around with the yogurt machines and scales. They called him "Yogi."

Nowadays, some of my best friends experience everything from entities knocking on the roof to get cleared from the earth plane, to seeing disease energetically in a person's body. It has mystified me why these anecdotes have always come my way.

In the past I did not solicit this information. People just start jabbering away. I haven't necessarily believed everything they've told me—but this material was coming into my life long before my "spiritual quest" as an adult.

In *The Celestine Prophecy,* the Seventh Insight states that everyone we meet has a message for us, and, conversely, we have a message for them. How can that be possible? Had people shared their experiences so I would remember who I am? To **Wake the Bleep Up?** On an unconscious level, had I been emitting a woo-woo vibe? Could my father have been wrong about spiritual stuff?

I'd soon find out. But, first, I had to get out of Massapequa, New York. *"Go West, Young Girl!"*

While the east coast was my original stomping ground, heaven on earth was called Colorado. By the time I was twenty, I knew that someday I would move west. A dozen years later, I settled near Boulder (home of Mork and Mindy), and it finally felt like I'd found my soul's true home.

My husband's work mentor invited us over for dinner one night. I immediately connected with his wife, Lisa, since she could remarkably sing the theme song from any late 60s TV show I could name. Though it seemed she had come into my life by coincidence, I had a strong feeling ours was not a haphazard encounter.

Lisa had left a graphic-design career to become a massage and body/mind therapist and knew numerous holistic-healing therapies. She's the one who introduced me to Jalynn, the intuitive. Our mutual interest in spirituality made us fast friends.

The following year, in 1995, Lisa offered me some metaphysical information that greatly influenced both of our lives. She handed me a few audiotapes from a channeled spiritual teacher named **Abraham**, whose teachings focus on a fundamental principle called the **Law of Attraction.** The nature of reality revealed! It's *tres* simple. *Like attracts like.* THE major reason I was on this bizarre rock-music journey.

What did this have to do with TBIF? The band certainly didn't seem interested in spiritual or metaphysical stuff. But sometimes, things aren't as they seem.

For years, I listened to dozens of the Abraham tapes. Over and over, they emphasize how our thoughts are vibration, and those vibrations draw situations and people to us—like magnets.

Quantum physicist Fred Alan Wolf (featured in the movies, *What The Bleep Do We Know?* and *The Secret*) uses a rock-music analogy to explain the Law of Attraction on his website:

> Do *like* things really attract each other? Actually, in quantum physics we find that *like* doesn't attract *like.... Like* charges repel each other (+ repels + and - repels -) and *unlike* charges attract (+ attracts -). The better metaphor might be **resonance**, that two things that vibrate together have more energy as compared to two things that vibrate out of phase with each other, in which case they have no energy.
>
> When you are attracted to another person, it is likely that you and the other are in some sense *vibrating in phase* with each other and each of you is *energized* more than just adding up your separate energies. It's more like **4** times the energy of each individual. With **3** persons, it goes as **9** times, and so on. Hence, large crowds rock at a concert together because those in attendance are each enormously energized by the presence of the others in *like* mindsets. Hence, the rock concert high....[6]

Let's break this down. Dr. Wolf's analogy offers one way of interpreting the Law of Attraction. Abraham generally focuses on using the Law to help us emotionally shift to a better feeling so we can manifest what we want in our life. Abraham presents three basic steps to creating with the Law of Attraction:

Ask for what you want. Keep in mind we don't always *ask* by speaking our desires. According to Abraham, asking more often "emanates" from us "vibrationally" as a constant stream of personally honed preferences, each building on the next....[7]

The Universe answers. No work on our part. This is up to the Big Cheese.

The answer given must be received and allowed. We've got to let it in. This is where we generally get stuck.

Through my attraction to rock music, I would come to discover a tremendous scope to the Law of Attraction—that it isn't simply our thoughts that attract experiences and people to us. It's much more than that.

The Law of Attraction has a very important component called **synchronicity.** The term *synchronicity* was used by Swiss psychiatrist **Carl Jung** to describe when universal forces align with the experiences of an individual and lead to coincidences that appear to be more than mere chance. Frequently, the synchronicity has a deeper meaning. According to Jung, such incidents happen because everything is innately connected and nothing occurs randomly. We draw certain people, situations, and experiences to us.

At first, I thought the Law of Attraction was a wad of metaphysical mumbo-jumbo, but I wound up having so many synchronicites about TBIF that it became obvious, even to me, that energetically we're all *connected* in some way, shape, or form.

Most of us experience coincidences, like when an old song that rarely gets airplay pops into our head as we climb into our car. Then we turn on the radio, and incredibly, that very song blasts from the speakers. We don't often ask ourselves, what does that mean? Why did this occur *now*? Is there a message I need to be aware of with the lyrics? Is my soul talking to me through this synchronicity?

To illustrate how the Law of Attraction and synchronicity work in tandem, I'll revisit the TBIF concert mentioned earlier, the one where I wound up in the second row.

I'd debated whether to go to the show because I couldn't get a decent seat, but news about VIP tickets spawned visions of a front-row spot. Through the beauty of *synchronicity*, my assigned seat was near the inebriated dude. Then the female security guard wanted to make sure I wasn't being harassed. I'm over six feet tall and I don't come across as a dainty waif, but, for whatever reason, she moved me from my crummy seat. The Universe had fulfilled my heart's desire.

Our vibration, or energy, must match the frequency of our desire to get the outcome we envision. We are like a radio receiver. If our signal doesn't match what we are asking, our desire won't be fulfilled.

In this case, my vibration *was* lined-up—because I had absolutely no expectations. I'd gone to the concert assuming my butt would be in the thirteenth row. I'd merely *envisioned* how nice it would be to be up front. In my experience, having no expectation—letting go—is by far the most difficult part of manifesting. We try to control how things will happen. Letting go is all about *surrender*. To let go of the outcome and *appreciate* whatever we've been given. You never know how things might turn out.

Here is an essential aspect of the Law of Attraction. Our mind isn't the exclusive cruise director of our life. Our *soul*—or higher consciousness—influences everything we do. As Carl Jung observed, a part of us *is* connected to everything, and seems to transcend time as well.

This higher consciousness often communicates with us through intuition. My soul saw the bigger picture...and *nudged* me to buy a ticket to that 1997 concert, despite the lousy seat.

Being close to TBIF in the second row sparked a feeling of connection with them—which eventually triggered a past-life recognition *and* an incredible spiritual journey. My deep desire to understand my attraction to TBIF then began to propel me into unexpected, but fascinating, territory: the nature of reality and human consciousness!

I've always been a big question asker. Also a huge whiner. I constantly grumbled to God about having no conscious memory of past lives. What's the point of experiencing past lives if I can't remember them? What was God smoking the day he decided to put the **veil of forgetfulness** upon the human race?

If reincarnation is real, why is the truth hidden from us? Wouldn't it help to end war and hatred if we remembered how we have behaved evil as well as kind? Been victimizer as well as the victim? I understand how total recall of every moment of every past life could make things a bit confusing, but could I at least have a hint as to who I was?

Despite having read many books that note various clues to our past lives—such as our attraction to geographic locations, time periods, and predilections—I was stuck for the longest time with a pissy attitude about my past lives. I knew lots of people who recalled their previous lifetimes. Why couldn't I remember mine?!

Asking God questions was a good thing. Staying ticked off, however, stymied my ability to channel for myself, to tap into my higher consciousness. I was a **psychic brick**. That's because *like attracts like*. Not only did remaining frustrated at the lack of connection with my higher self not solve anything; it created more annoyance and frustration for me. I kept thinking it was necessary to recall my past lives in order to gain insights. I ignored Abraham telling me to *let go* of *how* something would come into my life. *Just have the desire, and allow the Universe to orchestrate* *everything else.* All I had to do was remain open to whatever intuition might come my way, no matter how it appeared. But I was too attached to the format, so "Psychic Brick" became my middle name.

Despite my density, God must have heard my whiny complaints. Ultimately, when I least expected it, past life information did come through me...and bite me in the ass.

Shortly after my daughter was born in 1999, I asked the Universe (a.k.a. God), "Hey, can you give me an interesting subject to study while taking care of the beloved bambino?"

I visited a library one sunny day and a palmistry book caught my eye. *No, no, not palmistry. That's for quacks.*

But the book quacked at me, so I took it home. I discovered the lines of the hand are not just an arbitrary mishmash, but encoded messages about *us.* According to the art of **chiromancy (palm reading)**, experiences, health, and personality traits are embedded in the markings and lines of our hands via our **subconscious.**

Curious to see what my own hands revealed, I visited a palmist named Jan listed in the phone book. She started the session using astrology and hit on some of my life themes: "Your Saturn lies in the twelfth house, so you could literally channel your work. Writing a book, or being inspired by your dreams is very likely."

Yeah, right. Psychic Brick channel? Don't think so.

Then she looked at my hand and told me that my father, who died when I was sixteen, was now an architect on another planet and creates futuristic-looking geodesic dome houses.

That's ridiculous. Geodesic dome houses? Then again, after my father passed away, my mom told me he'd always wanted to be an architect, yet had never followed his life-long dream. And he *hated* antiques but loved futuristic looking furniture and artwork.

This kinda creeped me out. How'd she get that from the lines on my metacarpus? All right, psychic palm-reading lady, let's get back to the matter at *hand*—ME. What is the theme of *this* lifetime?

"The theme in this lifetime is about writing. In fact, every lifetime is about *writing*. Every life you are creating with words. This is the big lifetime, the last lifetime. This is the big hurrah!"

Big hurrah???? Writing?

Had she dialed into Hemmingway or Louisa May Alcott? I didn't know how to write a book anymore than I knew how to write a symphony. Besides, I had nothing to write about—until some weird, freaky stuff started happening around TBIF and their music.

TBIF came to the Denver area in August 2000. Eleven buddies accompanied me to the concert, which is amazing because several of my amigos think hard-rock music is for Neanderthals. One chum said, "I just want to see you make a fool of yourself in front of hundreds of people." She, of course, meant that in a nice way, since at a general admission show the reserved part of me really lets loose. Singing and bopping around in two inches of space in a standing-room only concert is about as wild and crazy as my suburban-mom lifestyle gets.

Jalynn, the intuitive, had become a friend over time. She courageously moved beyond her dolphin-and-whale CDs to see what this rock-music craze was all about. During the second half of the show, her eyes were closed and I yelled into her ear, "Everything okay?" She nodded. So I refocused my attention on the band, soaking up delectable aural delights.

When we left the Ogden Theater, Jalynn told me what she had experienced during the concert. "With my eyes closed, I saw images coming from the lead singer." She said a strong leader, father-like energy was emanating from him. She also saw an *orange* sky and a sine-wave pattern snaking across the horizon. When she asked her guides to explain what she was seeing, they replied: *The message is not for you.*

I stopped dead in my tracks. *Message not for you? DUH! The message is for me and the fans!*

Could TBIF really be emitting some kind of subconscious frequency with a hidden message? Yet *what* exactly are we supposed to **Wake the Bleep Up** to?

It had been several years since Jalynn saw the orange sky in the channeled reading about my past life with the band on another planet. Was it a coincidence that the palm reader had said my dad built futuristic buildings on another world? I felt like I'd stepped into the pages of a science fiction novel with intergalactic clues scattered all around: a cosmic musical jigsaw puzzle!

My intuition had nudged me once again. I'd never asked a bunch of TBIF virgins to attend a rock concert with me before. However, I asked, and friends came. Hey, asking is the first step of the Law of Attraction. I hadn't expected Jalynn to get all woo-woo and *see* something from the lead singer—but I *had* been asking the Universe to help me understand my attraction to the band. I had asked. One answer given: There is a hidden message in the band's music, specifically for their fans. Of course, even I knew that for the band it was all coming from their subconscious, or should I say higher conscious. They couldn't possibly be aware of this, could they?

Uh oh. What am I getting myself into?

CHAPTER 3
"LEAVE YOUR HAT ON"
—Joe Cocker

"It didn't matter to me that there were people, it didn't matter that I was shy. Just the sound was so captivating that it helped me to get rid of those inhibitions."[8]
—Eric Clapton, musician

The following night, TBIF played at a venue several hours away in Colorado Springs, which I attended alone. I struck up a conversation in the ladies room with a long-time fan of the lead guitarist. She remarked, "Whenever I go to a concert, I get right up front to the stage. It is very important that the guitarist notice me."

"Really? Why is that?" I asked, intrigued.

She wasn't quite sure.

I, too, wanted the band to notice me, which is why I wore my Superfan trademarked black sparkly hat. The hat had made its official debut several years earlier at a holiday party, but since it was so *sparkly,* there weren't many other opportunities for it to adorn my head—until a TBIF concert.

Around this time an acquaintance, Kathryn Severns, showed me a proposal for a self-help book she was writing titled *Tiara Training.* Little girls often dress up and wear tiaras, while waiting for their knight in shining armor to come and save them. Kathryn was asking women to reframe the childhood fantasy and become their *own* "knight." Part of the retraining process to increase self-esteem is to wear the tiara in public and not give a rat's ass about what others think. Cool!

So I continued wearing my sparkly hat in lieu of a tiara to the TBIF concerts, though it remained in my hand until the show started, so I wasn't advertising that I'm "Dork Girl." Wearing it is about as emotionally comfortable as wearing thong underwear woven from shards of broken glass.

I've worried about what other people think of me most of my life. Why? Because.

In the seventh grade, my body sprouted to six-feet tall. To say I was awkward is an understatement. *Retard, faggot,* and *gawk* were the favorite descriptors from my classmates. *Gawk* (a contraction of gangly and awkward) sent chills up my spine, because you had to be doofy *and* tall to earn that epithet in my neighborhood.

I had germinated in Massapequa, Long Island, affectionately referred to as "Matzo-Pizza" due to the high Jewish and Italian population. Jews and Italians aren't exactly the tallest folks in the world, which only made my blonde hair and skyscraper stature stick out even more. Thus, I was dubbed "Gawk Girl."

To top it all off, I never succumbed to peer pressure by smoking (except three times when I pulled a Bill Clinton and "didn't inhale"). Nor did I do drugs. It didn't take much to convince me that I'd either die from cancer or go to hell if either stuff touched my fingers. This made me all the more nerdly, though, and life was emotional torture.

Though the daily teasing abated by high school, I still believed what others had told me: I was pretty downright fugly. During my early teen years, the fear of rejection turned me into a shrinking violet. My sparkly hat was one tiny step toward being able to say, in my mind, to others: *Think whatever you want. I'm going to wear this silly sparkly thing on my noggin' that even the Village People would reject (and those guys really liked hats), so please keep your opinions to yourself.*

The point isn't whether or not we want to wear a tiara (men readers can substitute crown), but are we willing to move beyond the illusionary boundaries of "safe and acceptable" into "that's not cool" by other people's standards? Are our spines made of bricks or butter? Society's perceptions of conformity keep many of us in little imaginary boxes most of the time. For sixty minutes during TBIF concerts, I'd get up the courage to wear the hat, despite feeling like a total gawk.

The scintillating hat addressed my original concern that the band wouldn't see me in the audience. But the question still remained: Why did I care if TBIF knew I was there or not? Was being noticed by the band a form of egotism? Perhaps: "Hey Mom, look at me! A rock star recognizes *moi* out in the audience. Ka-ching."

But what if it wasn't just attention I longed for…but acknowledgment that we'd been together in a former life? Reincarnation research suggests that we hold memories of people from our past lives in our subconscious and that, if they are presently incarnated with us now, we can recognize their soul energy.

Over the years, as TBIF's popularity declined, their concerts were held in smaller venues. Sad for them, but great for me! I could get much closer to the musicians than I could at an arena concert—but vexatious feelings kept cropping up. My typical locale on the concert floor was at least a dozen feet back from the stage, with several fans in front of me, because it felt abnormal to be too close. I was often near enough to make eye contact, but I'd always avert my baby browns if they glanced my way.

Why, why, why does the band make me shy, shy, shy?

I couldn't envision myself trying to meet them, certain they would scream: "Oh, no! The giant lady with the sparkly hat! Run!" Where did this strange fear come from? A subconscious past-life memory? I had no idea at the time.

My Superfan attire might or might not have made an impression on the band, but it sure got the attention of fellow concertgoers. One tipsy woman at the Colorado Springs show said how much she liked my hat and commented several times about my tallness and that my skin looked nice. Her persistence gave me the heebie-jeebies.

Beauty is totally subjective, so I began to question its importance. If I were conventionally attractive, wouldn't the band have noticed me for more than a second? I felt invisible despite my sparkly hat.

So, I focused upon Jalynn's insight about TBIF having an intrinsic message encoded in their music, since Danae also had referred to their music as an encoded "wake-up" switch. **Wake the Bleep Up!**

It felt as though my DNA had been waiting for an enzyme (the bands's music) to come along and unlock my emotions and memories. But what if there was a dormant message in my DNA, and the band's music was the key to accessing it? What if the music was helping me to bring a cellular memory to the surface?

At the show in Denver, I had been on cloud nine. During the Colorado Springs show, I felt drastically different. No sense of connection with TBIF whatsoever. The band seemed more distant and far less into the music. It might have been my imagination, but I also sensed that one of the guys was intentionally avoiding looking at me. Maybe it was the hideous hat!

My drive home was somber and, about halfway during the two-hour ride, I began sobbing uncontrollably. *Why, why, why did that concert make me cry, cry, cry?*

I had an overwhelming feeling that I'd be letting down a lot of people by not grasping some very important information. Why had intuitives sensed a hidden message in the music? Was I the only fan on the planet who believed there might be something to it?

My desire to understand became a catalyst for my own personal growth. As I eased on down the Rock 'n' Roll Yellow Brick Road with the band, my sparkly hat sparked some deep emotions. This journey became a very long and winding one ever since, and at times, felt mostly uphill. Trying to figure out my issues with the band wasn't like taking a short stroll. It felt like I was ascending Mt. Everest in sandals and a bikini—completely unequipped for the challenge.

So, I phoned a different intuitive named Caron. "Do you see a past-life connection, if any," I asked, "with (name of guy in TBIF)?" I was dumbfounded by what she picked up. She saw a lifetime in the Middle East when he was a prince and I was his very young concubine. He had shunned me after our tryst, which had left me devastated.

I hung up the phone and couldn't believe that I'd possibly had a *relationship* with a band member in another life. *Ridiculous! I'm Gawk Girl from Matzo-Pizza, Long Island. What the hell am I doing hanging with a rock star formerly known as a prince?* What had happened to the tribal group energy Jalynn had sensed? It all seemed like pure fantasy. *Me, his concubine? No freakin' way.*

By the time I was twelve, motorcycles and electric guitars were my obsession. Anything girlish I quickly whisked off to the Salvation Army. *Wear a dress? Mom, I'd rather be ground up into tiny bits and fed to our cat.*

In junior high, my classmates' taunts had beaten out any shred of femininity left in my DNA, so I had totally morphed into a guy. I shut down all feelings of feminine power and relied on my masculine strength, both physically and intellectually, to survive.

Don't get me wrong, I liked boys, and I wanted them to like me—but tall, ugly, gawky girls don't get asked out by short school-aged guys. We get our books knocked out of our arms between classes, and we are ridiculed on a daily basis. In many cases, we're not even on their radar screen. We're invisible.

From afar, I watched the pretty girls get all the boys' attention. Yet there was something so weak about those girls that I was glad that would *never* be me. So, I acted and dressed like a dude, in the hopes that I'd be accepted. I figured, "If you can't beat 'em, join 'em," but deep down I prayed that someday the ugly duckling would transform into a beautiful girl swan—who could play like Clapton.

As I attended TBIF's concerts over the years, it felt like being dragged by the hair back into junior high. Lots of women were thrusting their cleavage toward the guys on stage. Why did some females use their bodies to manipulate and taunt, all for the sake of getting some attention from the band? It made my stomach turn into a big twisty knot.

While writing this book, a memory from high school resurfaced. I was hanging out on the bleachers with some girls, watching the boys' soccer-team practice. I made a risqué comment about one of the players. One of the girls jokingly remarked, loud enough for folks in Brooklyn to hear, "Oh, Laura, you're such a *whore!*"

WHORE?? Her words momentarily shocked and paralyzed me, like a jellyfish stinging its prey. I thought I was going to faint.

My reaction, however, made no sense. I never even had a date with a boy at that point. Though deep down I felt it was true.

Interestingly, years later, various intuitives have seen me either as a lady of the night, or extremely promiscuous in another life. And then a concubine. So it seems the girl in high school possibly had triggered an unconscious past-life memory. To balance past misuse of my femininity, had my soul chosen a more masculine body so I'd have to deal with my past **karma**?

On the other hand, I wondered, can't a woman's brains get her noticed? No way José. Not at a rock concert. In the history of rock 'n' roll, there has never been a male performer who looked into the audience and thought, "Oh, my God. That woman. She looks so *intelligent*. I *must* have a conversation with her! I can't wait to tell a roadie to bring her backstage after the show so we can *talk* about thermonuclear dynamics." Concerts are about embracing emotions, sensuality, and the physical realm, not our cerebral prowess.

Something was way out of whack in my brain. I wanted to be attractive to the band, but another part of me didn't want them to see me *at all. What the hell is wrong with me?* I wondered. These past-life readings and TBIF concerts were bringing up issues around my femininity and self-worth. No doubt about it.

One way I explored these emotionally challenging subjects was through my dreams. Ever dream about your favorite rock band while deeply asleep? I did, well over 100 times. And, no, these were not X-rated, "sex, drugs, and rock 'n' roll" reveries, but non-erotic communications cloaked in symbolism and metaphor from my subconscious mind. I'll give you a sneak-peak about one of my dreams with TBIF. But hold onto your sparkly hat—it involves popcorn.

CHAPTER 4
"WE ARE FAMILY"
—Sister Sledge

"We rarely hear the inward music, but we're all dancing to it nevertheless, directed by the one who teaches us, the pure joy of the sun, our music master."

—Rumi, thirteenth-century Persian poet and theologian

Many years ago, I dreamed that I was in a concert hall several hours before a TBIF concert. I was making popcorn and feeding it to the audience, but where was the band? I wanted to give popcorn to them too. But, no sign of them.

The day after the dream, I attended a session with the intuitive Caron. The first thing she said was, "I was told to ask you about the dream you had last night."

Shocked, I recounted the dream in detail. Then she quizzed me, "When you think of the band, what pops into your mind? What do they represent to you?"

Without hesitating, I blurted, "Power."

Until then, I hadn't realized that TBIF symbolized *power* in my subconscious, so I began looking at my dreams differently. What hidden messages in **symbolism** and **metaphor,** the language of my dreams, might I unearth?

For as long as I can remember, that which is "hidden" has enthralled me: fossils of dinosaur bones, single-celled amoebas, even hypnosis. The hidden metaphors and symbology in my dreams about the band seemed to be a perfect avenue for tapping into messages from my unconscious.

Sometimes dreams simply process our daily experiences. At other times, they tap into a vast collective of ancestral symbols known as **archetypes**, which offer clues and messages as to the direction we need to move in life. In his book *Dream Alchemy*, Ted Andrews says:

Symbols are the bridges between thinking and being. They provide messages about the world of reality around us. Because of this, most symbols speak figuratively and not literally. The symbology of your dreams will be couched in imagery that you can understand.[9]

I started journaling my dreams in 1999. By tracking my nocturnal wanderings over a period of time, patterns emerged and seemingly disparate themes started to make sense. One major theme that irked me was that in the vast majority of the 150+ dreams involving TBIF, I had little or no contact with the band. In many of the scenarios, a band member would be somewhere in the background, or the dreaded, "Oh my god, I got to the venue but missed the concert" dream would awaken me in a panic. How frustrating! For years, this pattern pissed me off.

There are numerous ways to interpret our nocturnal reveries. One common suggestion is to consider every element and person in a dream as an aspect of our self. After all, we create the scenes.

The intuitive Caron shared a process to interpret my dreams about TBIF. She said to ask myself, "Do they have a piece of music for your emotional state? Their being in your dream depends upon the emotional context of the dream. Music is part of your *feeling* body, so it helps you access your emotions."

Back to my popcorn dream, I recalled feeling stressed. I was trying to *give* something to the band, and to the fans.

Maybe I could find a connection to the popcorn symbology by rereading past journal entries where TBIF was in my dreams. I did see an association: I had rarely connected with or looked at them in the dreams (as well as during real concerts). Why? *Think, think, think. Oh thank you Pooh.*

My answer was in a psychology book by Carl Jung: The band was my **animus**. Ana who? The animus is the male counterpart of a female's psyche. In my subconscious mind, men have all the power, chicks don't.

Interestingly, over the years, there were a handful of dreams when I actually did connect with a band member. And guess what? The dreams generally involved one of the guys taking my hands and holding them, and I felt a wonderful wave of energy course through me. If the band represented my masculine self, what did this mean?

Their hands touching my hands symbolized connecting with my own power. It was about *me*—not them—the essential part of *me*. The dreams were letting me know that my power stems from *within*. TBIF represented my pattern of trying to *give it away*...give away my power. Popcorn, get your popcorn and discover your subconscious issues with a rock band!

Was I giving myself away solely from childhood issues, or might past lives also have created a fear around power?

Because the band symbolized power in my subconscious, I visited an intuitive in Boulder named Lee to see what *her* subconscious picked up. At the end of the session I asked, "Do you see any past lives with me and (name of guy in TBIF)?"

She saw us several centuries ago writing and working very hard together on a project. We were English revolutionaries and very passionate about our writing. Somewhere along the line, however, differences in our political and philosophical ideologies came between us and we ended our dynamic creative relationship, feeling betrayed by each other.

Lee noted that he was a part of my **soul family** and in this lifetime we were on the same spiritual path. Same spiritual path? Soul family? You've got to be kidding me! This seemed more outrageous than being his concubine.

The idea of being part of a rock band's "soul family" blew my mind, but was also extremely intriguing to me because Caron had said something similar months earlier: "Consider the band part of your oversoul." The **oversoul** is often defined as a family of related souls, like an etheric Partridge Family. But instead of this family travlin' along in an old colorful school bus, we're trying to get happy by healing our karmic issues with each other.

It might be helpful to review "soul" distinctions. Fortunately, I came across a fascinating book which explores the between-life state, *Journey of Souls*, by Dr. Michael Newton. Over several decades of working with clients in deep hypnosis, he classifies various soul associations in the nonphysical world. You've probably heard the term "**soul mate**" when two people have a recognition of each other, often through the eyes. Some people believe soul mates are your one-and-only true love, but they can also be souls that have "agreed to connect with you on this planet for a purpose. In some cases it is to clear up karma, in other cases it is to finish unfinished business, and for some, it is to accomplish a particular goal together."[10]

Companion soul mates frequently play important support roles in our lives. Dr. Newton's typical client had between three to five souls in their inner circle. **Affiliate souls** are members of secondary groups and can total a thousand souls or more. Some affiliated soul groups work with us through many lifetimes; others may cross our path only briefly. Parents often come from one of these nearby cluster groups.

According to Newton, an affiliate soul might have a specific characteristic that is exactly what we need to bring a karmic lesson into our life. They are usually people who carry a strong positive or negative energy in their association with us. In your own life, think about people you were close to over the years (or people you despise). Chances are you were together before in some other lifetime. This concept is acknowledged in most rein-carnation studies.

I believe that some of the guys in TBIF are *most likely* from the same soul cluster as me. Could part of their affiliated soul group be comprised of people who are their hardcore fans today?

At one of Dr. Newton's lectures, a psychiatrist in the audi-ence said the discussion on soul groups reminded him of tribal-ism. Newton says that soul groups do appear to be tribal in their intense loyalty and mutual support for each other in a spiritual community; however, they don't act nastily toward other groups the way humans often do. Among souls, there is great respect.

This reminded me of Jalynn's comments regarding my past life when she saw me and TBIF as a clan or tribe. Are fans who are passionate about a band and their music displaying an intense tribal loyalty because of a past life soul affiliation?

In my earlier radio jobs, I had studied demographics and clusters of people based upon where they lived and how their lifestyles were similar. Now I wondered how all this coordination happened—so that a soul incarnates into the right body, with the perfect family, in the needed geographic location, giving the soul an opportunity to proceed with its life purpose.

This would be important in music, because rock-band members sometimes come together from the same town or neighborhood. For example, The Beatles made Liverpool, England famous; REM and the B-52's put Athens, Georgia on the map; and the guys in TBIF all stemmed from the same town in Illinois. What are the staggering odds that young musicians from the middle of nowhere end up having such incredible synergy and discover each other? The Law of Attraction!

As for geography, Newton wrote, "Although souls typically do not incarnate in the same hereditary family they had in past lives, members of the same soul group most definitely choose new families where they can be together. Members of soul groups tend to be associated in each life by blood ties and geographic proximity."[11] Based upon this premise, incarnating rock musicians often need to arrange for their amigos to be in the same geographic vicinity, so they have a greater likelihood of hooking up.

Many reincarnation studies suggest that people are drawn to a geographic area due to a past life there. I had been drawn to Colorado since my late teens.

Our soul pulls us to the places we need to be, so that our life path can unfold even if we weren't born in the precise location. With friends in Colorado, I have formed some of the closest spiritual bonds I've ever felt.

The following Internet excerpt discusses the concept of the oversoul, and suggests another possible reason people may be drawn together:

> Most souls who exist today were cloned or split off of some of these ancient primal souls (your Spiritual Parents). Members of this ancestry are considered to be part of an oversoul grouping or soul family, having originally shared in a single consciousness and identity.
>
> The Spiritual Parent and Oversoul (in its entirety) is analogous to (at one time) being a whole mirror... imprinted with the one image of the Creator. Imagine this mirror being fractured...split off into bits and pieces, scattered throughout the universe...yet the one image (with some slight distortion) is holographically seen on each splintered portion of the mirror. In other words, all the

people of this Oversoul grouping will mirror or "reflect" your original soul (more or less), showing you some image (from various perspectives) of the parental being from whence you came. These souls will always feel an "affinity" to those other souls who came from the same spiritual parents.

This "affinity" is expressed in the concept of "soul mates"—which are all those beings who are in your "over-soul" family....[12]

The oversoul description of a fractured mirror immediately brought to mind one of TBIF's album covers. Each guy's face is shown in overlapping square mirrors. Yet on the back jacket, there is a full-body shot and each musician is holding up a mirror that reflects the face of a different band member. I feel as though TBIF is *my* mirror. Through them, by attending their concerts, I get reflected back to me the hidden parts of myself that I couldn't see before.

There are entire books and many websites that explore the nature of the soul, but I can't tell you what's valid or not. I look for consistency among sources and try to assess whether the information jibes with my own experience—and I keep an open mind. Whether or not the term "oversoul" is accurate, what is most important to comprehend is how "group consciousness" impacts our lives. Dead or alive, we're all a bunch of *groupies*.

So *this* groupie took a moment to review the various past-life scenarios per the intuitives. Jalynn had seen me as part of a warrior clan on another planet. Danae felt that TBIF is part a large soul group, and their music triggers an encoded spiritual wake-up switch in some fans. Caron sensed a tragic relationship between a concubine and a prince in the Middle East. Then Lee picked up on me and the rock star as writing collaborators in Old

England, who felt betrayed by one another. Did any common themes parallel my current lifetime?

As a possible warrior on another planet, it wasn't simply the Thor connection that got my attention. In *this* lifetime, I'm a freakin' Amazon (minus the humongo breasts). But instead of physically grinding men into tender chewy chunks, I'm transforming into a *spiritual* warrior.

The rejection/betrayal theme also stood out. Definite thread there. My dreams suggested that I had issues surrounding power and self-worth. TBIF's concerts brought up my complexes around sexuality and femininity. Lee said there was something to heal between me and a band member from the lifetime as a writer. So perhaps the soul family concept had some credence— since our *family* tends to trigger our issues.

I needed to be a spiritual warrior to discover the truth about my soul family. Yet becoming a warrior doesn't happen overnight. Lots of metaphysical things still frightened me. Like the phantasmagorical supernovas to come!

CHAPTER 5

"THE FUTURE'S SO BRIGHT"

—Timbuk3

"For me, music is always the language which permits one to converse with the Beyond."

—Robert Schumann, German Romantic composer

My next TBIF concert wasn't quite a supernova. More of a super no-show. The band was scheduled to perform in Spokane, Washington, about two hours from where I was vacationing with relatives. Psyched to see the guys in the band again, I got my ass to Spokane, but the lead singer had some kind of sore throat/cold thingy and sounded like he'd swallowed a large green amphibian. The guys attempted to go on with the show, but after a few songs it became apparent that Froggie's vocals weren't going to improve, so they made their apologies and hopped off the stage. Ribbit. Ribbit.

I leaped off my lily pad, over to the merchandise booth, and bought a copy of their latest DVD from their merchandise manager. Back in 1998, I'd met him during the band's **Three Night Stand** series of concerts in Boulder, when I had arrived, "stupid early" of course. Bored and with no one to talk to, I approached the merchandise table and we struck up a conversation about T-shirts and life on the road with the band. He had been with them for eons. For the first time in my nearly two decades of fandom, someone who really knew TBIF shared a few personal stories about them. Suddenly they weren't just rock stars but real people to me.

Now, three years later in Spokane, things felt different. This concert was outdoors and throngs of fans bustled about the merchandise tent. I purchased the DVD without speaking to the merch guy. He seemed a shadow of his former self, tired and distant, even melancholy. Several months later, I was saddened to learn that he had passed away from cancer.

When reading about his death on the band's website, a pang of loss enveloped me. My father had also succumbed to cancer when I was sixteen. The merchandise man had an only child, a daughter, who was that same age. My heart was in my throat. I too was an only child. The parallels felt symbolic, almost predestined. As it turned out, the merchandise man would become a mentor in a way I never dreamed possible.

Several months after the Spokane show, TBIF announced they were coming to Denver as the opening act for Aerosmith. Yippie! But it was in the gargantuan 19,000-seat Pepsi Center, and by the time TBIF was added to the bill, all that remained were nosebleed seats. Crap. Now that I'd been to lots of TBIF concerts in smaller, general-admission venues, it felt like 1997 again. I was weighing the pros and cons of attending—"should I stay or should I go?"—when something went bump in the night and shocked the bejesus out of me.

While lying in my dark bedroom one night, contemplating my ticket dilemma, the deceased merchandise manager came to mind. I wondered if it was possible to communicate with him since my psychic buddies claimed that anyone could connect with someone's soul after they have passed on, through focus and intention or meditation. If my compadres could do it, why not me? So I figured it wouldn't hurt to ask a few questions.

But before long my thoughts drifted to my dad. The fact that they both had cancer probably triggered the association. Suddenly, emotions gushed out of me like a Yellowstone geyser.

Great sorrow overwhelmed me and I silently cried so as not to wake my husband. I grieved that my daughters wouldn't know their grandfather, and I told my dad how much he would have enjoyed being with them. I hoped he could energetically connect with them.

My questions ping-ponged between merch man and my dad: What's it like where you are? Are you in a similar place? How can I better connect with you? Can you eat chocolate cheesecake in heaven?

Faster and faster, questions flew from my mind, creating a torrent of emotions that grew into a cyclone of energy, when I heard—**BANG!!**—a huge pop, followed by a crackling noise with the intensity of a gunshot. A bright blue light flashed from my bathroom ten feet away. I bolted from the bed, but I didn't see or hear anything else. What was that? An etheric supernova? At first I thought my imagination had gotten the best of me—but I definitely wasn't asleep when it happened.

About a month later, I got my answer. I read a book that described when a nonphysical entity pierces through into the physical realm, it creates a loud popping noise, like a spark being ignited.

Aaargghh matey, well, blow me down. Ain't that interestin'? Maybe Gawk Girl couldn't talk to or see the dead, like her psychic amigos, but she had experienced some kind of paranormal phenomena, nonetheless!

Could I reproduce my emotional and intellectual state of mind and recreate the sound and light manifestation? Probably not. Science would say it was simply a fluke—but something had taken place…and it wasn't all in my pretty little head.

I noticed that it was sound that got my attention. Sound, like in vibration. What a perfect way for the deceased to say, "Hi, we are here. Do you hear us?"

But back to my ticket dilemma and the upcoming Aerosmith/TBIF show. Like millions of other teens in the late 1970s, I too had dug Aerosmith's music. They had been scheduled to play at the Nassau Coliseum on Long Island, and I'd considered going, but only the coolest kids went to their concerts back then. Since the cool gene was horribly mutated in my own DNA, I had reluctantly decided not to attend. Instead, I had opted to irritate my mother and practiced the French horn all night.

Nearly a quarter of a century later, I didn't give a flying fat rat's fanny about fitting in. So, I caved and purchased a seat in the upper stratosphere and joined the legions of Aerosmith fans on that fateful, cold January night.

When TBIF performed, the man sitting next to me generously offered his binoculars since I didn't have a funky bionic eyeball. Now I could see the guys, who were seven light-years away. After having watched the band up close and personal so often, this sucked big time. Yes, my snooty nose lifted into the cirrus clouds. I was spoiled rotten.

But things are not always as they seem. Maybe I was supposed to be in a crappy seat, since the guy with the binoculars is possibly the reason why this book exists. After TBIF's set, while we waited for Steve Tyler and friends to come on stage, Binocular Guy mentioned all the free tickets he was receiving for concerts through his work. A recent Def Leppard performance had greatly impressed him. "I've never been to a concert where the fans were so into the music," he said. "It was like everyone in Red Rocks amphitheater was singing every word to every song."

The Law of Attraction had landed me next to a perfect stranger whose words would change my life. Say what???

The Celestine Prophecy says that every person we meet has a message for us, even a dude with binoculars at a rock concert.

One night, several weeks after the Aerosmith show, bambina

number two was contentedly slurping down breast milk as I rocked her in my arms. Thoughts about Binocular Guy's comments regarding Def Leppard fans came to mind. Why were those fans still so passionate about the music? What exactly did they feel drawn to?

A metaphoric two by four whacked me upside the head. If I possibly had past lives with TBIF, what about the fans of other bands, like Def Leppard? Could their fans be compelled to see them in concert because they too have had past lives together? If a rock group incarnates with the intention of bringing large groups of people together again, through the Law of Attraction, what were the implications?

I had been asking the Universe to help me understand my attraction to TBIF. Tonight, I begged, *Tell me, Universe, why are so many fans compelled to follow their favorite bands for several decades? This isn't normal behavior for middle-aged people. What on earth is wrong with us?*

Ask, and it is given.

In the next moment, my life was forever altered. The words **Group Soul Reincarnation** reverberated from deep within my psyche, accompanied by an intense explosion of energy throughout my body, and a wave of heat coursed through me. In that moment, time ceased to exist. Everything was now. My ego totally dissolved. Past and future collapsed into the present...and I was lifted into another dimension of insight.

A knowing washed over me and in that instant, I knew I had written a book about group reincarnation and rock music that delivered an uplifting message to an audience not typically reached by spiritual concepts. That text already existed and was as real as any book on my nightstand...and it had a significant impact on the people of my generation—other rockers, just like me.

I felt as if I had entered a parallel universe. Everything was absolutely surreal.

After several seconds, my senses returned and I hugged my daughter. Thank heavens she was real! I touched her crib and the walls of the bedroom. Solid as a rock. Everything had returned to normalcy…except me.

"WHAT THE BLEEP JUST HAPPENED?"

An inner light had switched on, one trillion watts of electrical euphoria, bliss, ecstasy, and joy consumed me. How could I possibly know something beyond amazing would happen to my generation? But I did. The future's so bright, we gotta wear shades.

This perpetual state of bliss lasted many months and I never doubted what I knew that night. I had written a book. Past tense. Yet my logical mind couldn't make heads or tails of this. How on earth could something like this occur? Was I a complete freakazoid? Had anyone else ever experienced a similar kind of mystical awakening?

Ask, and it is given.

I eventually found research confirming that my mystical adventure was not all that unusual. Abraham Maslow, one of the founders of humanistic psychology, describes a similar phenomenon as a **peak experience**. Near-death researcher P.M.H. Atwater calls it a **future memory episode**. These experiences often involve a sense of bliss. In the case of a future memory episode, great swells of vitality and an insatiable desire to learn accompany a vision of seeing the future.

"Insatiable desire to learn" puts it mildly. After my awakening to this inner force and identity beyond Gawk Girl, my hunger for knowledge was voracious. I was consumed by an overwhelming urge to absorb everything about physics and spirituality, group past-life studies, the Tarot, sacred geometry, alchemy, numerology, the harmony of the spheres…and the hidden power of music.

My mind went ballistic. Dozens of books were strewn all over my house. Many volumes I seemed to swallow whole—on topics that had never appealed to me before. Weird thing was (as if this wasn't weird enough) long-forgotten childhood memories started to uncontrollably spill out of me. I jotted them down into my computer, and spent the remainder of my spare time being a mom to my two young daughters.

It took eons of time to realize that I was on a journey of self-discovery. My soul had simply given me one important clue to follow: group soul reincarnation. It was like a little Cadbury chocolate bar with caramel filling, dangling from a string in front of my face, prodding me to follow it. Chase the little reincarnation carrot. The reward of the journey might be fattening for my body, but it certainly would transform my soul.

Was I actually remembering what would happen? Back to the Future, I guess. In *Future Memory*, Atwater concludes that "future memory is not some incredulous anomaly, but instead, shows that one's brain structure and brain capacity can indeed change. Such a change…leads to a greater awareness of life's meaning and spiritual purpose."[13] And discover life's meaning I would. I had no idea at the time what wonderful surprises my soul had in store for me as I stumbled down this Rock 'n' Roll Reincarnation Yellow Brick Road.

CHAPTER 6

"How Do You Drive Helen Keller Crazy?"
Put her in a round room and tell her the door is in the corner.

—Eighth-grade joke

"You can't describe it [playing rock music] except to say it's like a mysterious energy that comes from the metaphysical plane and into my body. It's almost like being a medium...."[14]

—Marc Storace, musician

At this juncture, you'd might as well have called me *Tommy*, the deaf, dumb, and blind kid. Intuitively, I was still blind as a bat and deaf as a post. Unlike the kid in *The Sixth Sense*, I don't see dead people or auras or sense energy. I don't predict the future. So why was I was given this mystical job?

Aside from my own future memory episode (an unintended spontaneous experience), the whole thing seemed ludicrous. I'd never written a book before. To top it off, I was supposed to write about group reincarnation and rock music? For the love of God, what soul came up with *that* brilliant idea? Perhaps I should just be put away *before* my daughters learned to ask, "Where are they hauling Mommy off to in that white jacket?"

So I had a talk with the Universe: *Hey, God, it's me, Laura. Yes, the tall one in Colorado. So you want me to write a book about group reincarnation and rock music and put my name on it? Are you completely loco? They'll tar and feather me. If you want me to do this, I'm game, but I need help. Please show me the path. Give me courage and insight to know what to do and what to write. Guess I've gotta have faith.*

My birth family name Faeth, pronounced "faith," can't be an accident. Keeping the faeth throughout this journey would damn near kill me.

Only one thought gave me resolution and strength to overcome my fears and doubts. Maybe such a book would help spiritually awaken those still asleep in my generation? I *knew* there would be a day when the future's so bright we gotta wear shades. So onward I trekked.

For months after my mystical mind-warp, it felt like someone had sawed off the top of my head and dumped in thousands of concepts, insights, and memories. I could barely keep up with the manic pace of information downloading into my brain.

As these dumpings increased, words like **archetype** continually plagued my every waking moment. Archetypes are a bit difficult to explain, but the guy who put synchronicity on the map, **Carl Jung,** described them as stemming from our **collective unconscious**. Jung feels that archetypes are inherited memories represented in the mind as universal symbols, and can be observed in dreams and myths…. Archetypes are universal constructions of psychic energy. They exist as potential and lie dormant in your consciousness.[15] I think of them as energetic blueprints that each of us has imprinted upon our psyche.

Familiar archetypes include Mother, Father, Hero, Trickster, Goddess, Wise Old Man, and Child. But what's really cool is that archetypes are hidden *templates* that shape and influence our experiences.

Jung's belief that archetypes are universal to all humans told me that each of us taps into these energies via our subconscious, often through our dreams, as mentioned earlier. Archetypes may address how our personal preferences develop. I suspect that it isn't entirely from environmental influences or our genetic make-up. Perhaps proclivities from past lives play a role. Past-life memories might imprint archetypal patterns on our subconscious, answering why we prefer redheads whereas our brother digs brunettes. Or why when I was only four years old blond, long-haired Thor was totally dreamy but clean-cut Peter Parker, Bruce Wayne, and Captain America just didn't rev my engine. Was it a coincidence that the lead singer of TBIF looked so much like Thor to me? Was that in part what drew me to the band? Or had his image been impressed into my psyche from other lifetimes?

All this thinking. Ow, Ow, OW! My poor little cranium was about to split open. Somebody please get me a mega dose of Excedrin right away! This brain expansion is killing me!

My next pressing question revolved around numbers, particularly the number four. Like archetypes, this number kept repeating itself in my mind, so I figured it was an important clue. Does "four" have anything to do with rock 'n' roll? Well, yeah. A typical band has four members: a guitarist, bassist, drummer, and vocalist.

But there was something deeper. Why had those particular instruments become the staples of rock music? What unique *vibrations* do the guitar, bass, and drum emit that turns fans into moths around a flame? There seemed to be an important link here that my little cerebellum couldn't grasp, and it took some time to uncover the clues that would help to answer these questions.

The possibility that fans were drawn to a musician or a band on some level—because they fulfilled an archetype—kind of mystified me. According to Carl Jung, "Archetypes create myths, religions, and philosophical ideas that influence and set their stamp on whole nations and epochs."[16]

Yikes. That's pretty heavy stuff. Rock musicians certainly have set their stamp on whole nations. So let's explore what archetype TBIF might be fulfilling for fans.

The singer and bassist fulfill the role of fetching heart-throbs. In contrast, the drummer and guitarist epitomize Average Joe. Early in their career, TBIF's guitarist played upon this trait and actually went to an extreme by dressing and acting goofy. While other rock stars had big poofy hair, tight leather pants, and *cool* oozing out of every pore, he let his guitar and lyrics make a statement. The contrast among the players was like *light* against *dark*.

Could the band archetypally represent **Dr. Jekyll and Mr. Hyde?** Might the singer's blond hair compared to the bassist's darker locks represent the light and the dark? Hyde's name is obviously a play on words, *hide*, since the dark is *hidden* within the doctor and symbolic of the Jungian archetype we all carry, the shadow. The **shadow** represents the darker, unconscious part of our nature that we've pushed away and keep *hidden* from the world. Sniff sniff. I smelled a clue.

What's dark and light and read all over? Oh, my heavens. A major symbol (dark and light) right under my nose! TIBF's MOTIF: alternating black-and-white checkered squares. The checkerboard had been a part of their guitars, merchandise, and albums for as long as I could remember. Merely a design element, right? Sometimes things aren't always what they seem.

Then a fan on TBIF's message boards asked if anyone else thought the lead guitarist reminded them of the Wizard in *The Wonderful Wizard of Oz.* Now, here was a thought-provoking question. She regarded him as the guy behind the curtain, weaving his magic without anyone realizing who ultimately was controlling all of the power. Was the guitarist, like the wizard, *hiding* his true identity? I wondered. This post gave me hope that others were tapping into how the band represented an archetype, or myth, and I thanked the Universe and the Law of Attraction for bringing me this confirmation.

Exploring human archetypes seemed to be sending me into an alternate reality. Like Dorothy, I felt like I was being catapulted into a very bizarre, unknown land. Had I traded "popcorn dreams" for hallucinogenic poppies?

Yet I sensed I was onto something important. Maybe God did give me the right assignment after all?

Lions and tigers and self-discovery. Oh, my.

CHAPTER 7

"ANCIENT WARRIOR"

—Black Sabbath

*"When we go into the inner chamber and shut the door to
every sound that comes from the life without, then will the
voice of God speak to our Soul and we will know the
keynote of our life."*[17]

—Hazrat Inayat Khan, founder of Universal Sufism, musician, mystic

Help, I need somebody. HELP!

Archetypes. Wizards. Hidden messages in music. Where
would I go from here?

It was time to consult with intuitive Danae again for some
direction. I launched with a question about a particular TBIF
member. "What lifetimes have I had with (name) that are important for me to know?"

"I see two children in Scotland," Danae said. "He's a boy and
you're a girl. You're in a clearing in the woods. It's a secret place
the two of you know. He seems to be more of a teacher, even
though you are about the same age. You share an art that is of a
mystical nature. You're creating emanations. For example, you say
ahhhh and it crystallizes as a physical symbol. What you are doing
is tickling each other, for this is the pure language of sound. It's
similar to when twins are in the womb together. It's as if you both
share this secret language, like twins. It fades with the years, but
you did have that bond with each other."

Making physical symbols with our voice was a new concept
to me. I'd never heard of such a thing. However, Danae's com-

ments about a pure language of *sound* reminded me of my childhood when each note on the piano had a certain role. In my mind, C was a Queen, G the King, and all the other notes spoke to each other. Each had a distinct personality because of its unique vibration and tone. Told ya' I was an odd child.

"Danae, do you see any other pertinent lifetimes with the soul of the guy from TBIF?" I asked.

"The next image is not from earth. You are spiritual warriors in a ship off-planet. You are brothers and you're very close, psychically attuned, and fighting for the light. There is a true kinship, but I don't know what you're fighting for. It's something about liberating a population of people. You are afloat together, and you both know you are about to die. You bow as warriors to one another energetically. There is a deep soul riveting. You did what you came to do and there is a feeling of completion. In this lifetime, there is a feeling of draw between your souls to complete something, to bring something forward."

A warrior on another planet? That's what Jalynn saw years ago. I then asked about the soul group.

"The band soul group moves with the vibrational wave of their music," Danae continued. "What you feel is akin to the calling. Soul groups are moving as armies of light to bring forward this new millennium…. Understand, not everybody in the soul group has a conscious awareness of the call. It is possible that even the band is not consciously aware of their doings."

I don't get it. Our soul group is an army of light, yet the band and no one else is conscious of this little important piece of information except ME? What's going on? And I'm a female, for crying out loud. Shouldn't this information come from a guy, since rock music was originated by dudes?

"Okay, Danae. I'm a woman attracted to rock music, and I want the scoop. I've been curious about this since my radio research days. Why does rock music seem to primarily appeal to men? And what makes women who relish rock 'n' roll different from the rest of the population?"

"It is the archetype of the warrior," she replied. "The women who carry the vibration of the warrior will resonate with rock music more than women who do not carry the warrior spirit. For men, it is ancestral history going back to the age of cavemen, when the warrior spirit was the heartbeat of the drum. It calls them into march."

Warriors *again*. Perhaps my joke about being an Amazon warrior wasn't so far-fetched. I liked the idea of being an army of light. It made me feel all angelic. But what about the sounds of rock 'n' roll instruments?

"Why are fans drawn to instruments like the drum, electric guitar, and bass?" I asked.

"The instruments," she answered, "resonate with the lower chakras—first, second, and third—which open up the rooting to the planet, grounding to the earth."

What's a chakra? Glad you asked. Here's the *Reader's Digest* answer:

Chakras are generally described as spinning energy centers of light. We don't see chakras with our eyeballs, but with our innersight, or mind's eye. Seven primary chakras are located along the spine and head. Each chakra corresponds to various emotional and physical states. When the energy of one or more chakras is out of balance, physical symptoms may manifest in a corresponding part of the body (see online glossary for more details).

After the first three chakras, which are associated with security (base of the spine), creativity and sexuality (sexual organs), and who we are in the world (solar plexus), we move to the heart chakra (the fourth chakra). The heart chakra is the transition point between the three lower and three upper chakras. It is linked to unconditional love of self and others and can be a bridge to transcendent states of consciousness. If rock music primarily stimulates our three lower chakras, I wonder if it does so in order to help open our heart? Maybe that's why so many rock-music lyrics focus on *love*?

I asked Danae how rock music impacts different people. She said, "The resonance of the lower chakras [grounded in the physical, material world] is irritating for someone who is drawn to the upper chakras [representing the spiritual realm]."

That made me laugh so hard that the walls shook and a poster of TBIF flew to the floor. No wonder I was so flippin' confused about my attraction to rock music AND spirituality. I was a spiritual seeker, yet the music didn't sound one iota mystical. It appears I'm an oxymoron, but maybe it's genetic.

I was curious if I was attracted to rock music because it's encoded in my DNA. Danae said it is cellular memory from many lifetimes. I did not take that to mean that my ancestors listened to rock music, but that the sound of the drum and primal rhythms were passed down generation to generation.

Then she said something that surprised me. She noted that we carry in our physical features the emotions, mental memories, and experiences of our past lives.

Fascinating! Our faces reflect our personality and past experiences. Maybe that's why some people seem so familiar even though we've never met? We've seen them in another life! As with many of the clues I was uncovering, "face reading" would come up again later in my journey.

But right now, I wanted to understand more about music and why it was impacting me so strongly. "What exactly do artists create with their words and music?" I asked.

"They are creating a sound, a vibrational standing resonance. For example, pluck a guitar string and it goes boinnnggg. It ripples out into the ethers and creates a wave of movement. When we propel our consciousness into form, whether physical art or musical art, we cause an effect upon the ethers, a resonance…a sound wave."

"When something is recorded," Danae continued, "and that sound can be played over and over again, that resonance continues, a **standing wave**, repeating the cause and effect of the sound. It comes from cause and has an effect upon listeners vibrationally. It is almost a living consciousness."

Wow. Music's vibration, coupled with our thoughts, creates a standing wave. Caron also had told me music could change my biochemistry. This was intriguing.

"Are you saying," I asked Danae, "that music creates a wave that changes us energetically?"

"Yes. If you're trying to change a brain-wave pattern or change a belief system, let's say you have an alpha tape you play over and over again. Your brain registers the vibration of the new material, and your mind records the new thought forms. There are many levels on which the music operates. So, regardless of subject matter, any song you feed yourself over and over feeds a new script into your being."

In my popcorn dream, I had been "feeding" the audience and the band my power. Music appears to feed and nourish us on numerous levels, so sound must be high-octane vibrational food for my soul.

This reading contained lots of material to digest. Burp. Ahh, that feels better. Now I've got room to digest the next tasty course on my journey—group reincarnation.

CHAPTER 8

"REAL GOOD FRIENDS"

—Blessid Union of Souls

"I think my fans will follow me into our combined old age. Real musicians and real fans stay together for a long, long time."[18]   —Bonnie Raitt, musician

I'd read numerous reincarnation books over the years, but never any about group reincarnation. Did this even exist? To my surprise, it does!

Mission to Millboro and *Return to Millboro* by Marge Rieder, Ph.D., *Earthly Purpose* by Dick Sutphen, and *A Tribe Returned* by Margaret Cunningham, Ph.D., relay hypnotherapists' case studies of past-life sessions in which the subjects all lived during the same lifetimes. The Millboro group had lived together in Virginia during the Civil War. *Earthly Purpose* focuses on hundreds of people who recall being in Teotihuacan, Mexico, 1,400 years ago. In *A Tribe Returned*, about thirty people remember their lives as Dakota Oglala American Indians.

In each case, the people related memories in their own points of view—from the past lifetimes. These memories provided the pieces of these puzzles by which each therapist assembled a story of what had transpired for their soul group. Incredibly, each group of stories jibed, even though some of the participants didn't know each other in *this* lifetime.

All of the past-life memories center on tragedy. In *Return to Millboro*, a much-loved woman in the small town of Millboro during the Civil War was raped and murdered. In *Earthly*

Purpose, 25,000 people were buried alive due to religious and political conflicts. *A Tribe Returned* reiterates events leading up to the massacre of a tribe of American Indians by white soldiers. Another book, *We Are One Another,* focuses on eight people who remember a lifetime as a Gnostic religious sect known as the **Cathars.** During the thirteenth century, this group was burned at the stake.

My heavens, what an absolute trauma fest! Gruesome and horrific. The question "Why?" haunted me. Why are human beings so horrendous to one another? Why does such suffering go on? These stories triggered my own childhood fears of war and mass annihilation, to the point that I couldn't even read all the details.

The books shed light on the power of past-life recall and how we all play various roles in our worldly drama. What if we *relive* the same dynamic repeatedly? I wondered. Do we do this until we tire of the pain and learn from our suffering?

Can we choose a different course of action? I hope so, because one definition of insanity is doing or thinking the same thing over and over again and expecting a different outcome. I believe that we collectively continue to make the same choices because our ego (our shadow) keeps us locked in a perpetual loop.

Is it possible to evolve past thousands of years of fear, hate, and mistrust? Did the band's black-and-white checkerboard motif symbolize not only light and dark, but good versus evil? I wondered if I was attracted to TBIF because I was trying to heal some traumatic incident from another life. Why else did the words "group reincarnation" rip apart the fabric of my consciousness? Had to have *faeth* that all of these past-life suppositions would eventually make sense.

Two other books, *Ripples* (retitled *Souls Don't Lie*) by Jenny

Smedley and *Loving Mozart* by Mary Montaño, attracted my attention because they present personal accounts of two women with past-life recalls with famous musicians. Seeing country-music performer Garth Brooks for the first time on television had triggered deep unconscious memories in Jenny Smedley. She vividly recalled a lifetime with him during the seventeenth century, which had caused her great heartache. The traumatic experience impacted her *today*. Jenny, who is English, wrote on her website that healing the painful memories with Garth changed her from a "suicidal and overweight housewife, with apparently no talent and no future, into a successful, happy author, screenplay writer, newspaper and magazine columnist, song writer, and TV presenter"[19] of her own show.

Mary Montaño remembered being Franz Xaver Sussmayr, beloved friend and collaborator of Wolfgang Amadeus Mozart during the last three years of his tragic life. Her description of Mozart's final months, where he was dying in physical and emotional agony, is excruciatingly painful to read. Talk about heartache!

Stock up on Kleenex if you decide to read any of these reincarnation stories. They are not light summer reading since the above-mentioned books focus on good versus evil. Yet amidst the sorrow and pain, comes a message eternal that gives us hope: We return over and over again to a physical body, because our previous traumas become *vibrationally encoded* in our soul. Even death does not alleviate karmic pain and suffering.

Apparently, the phrase, "You can't take it with you," does not apply to our spirit. Like a shadow, karma follows us lifetime to lifetime—until we restore inner harmony and balance in our life.

In *Earthly Purpose*, Dick Sutphen states, "Knowledge of your past lives can help you to understand what *influences, restricts,* or *motivates* you in the present. My investigation of what happened in Teotihuacan 1,400 years ago has helped me to understand my passions—to secure freedom, to battle repression, and to empower others to help themselves."[20]

Our past traumas, whether from this lifetime or another, impact who we are *right now*—unless we heal them. I sense that music can help us bring our traumatic emotions from the past to our conscious awareness, so we may transmute our pain into power.

One reason I believe that we unconsciously hold onto our emotional pain is because it is encoded in an essential element in our bodies: water.

Dr. Masaru Emoto's book, *The Hidden Messages in Water*, is a high-speed photographic study of crystals formed in frozen water, revealing changes when specific, concentrated thoughts were directed toward them. In one experiment, he had taped the words "Love and Gratitude" onto a glass of water and the words "You Fool" onto another glass of water from the same source. The photographs are astounding! The "Love and Gratitude" water created a beautiful hexagonal crystal; the "You Fool" water created no crystals at all. Incredibly, it didn't matter in which language the words were written or spoken. The results were always the same.

Dr. Emoto also studied the impact of music on water. Depending on the words spoken or the music played, the water took on the characteristics of its influence. For example, water that *listened* to Elvis Presley's *Heartbreak Hotel* formed a crystal divided into two parts, mimicking a heart breaking in two. When the water listened to Gospel music, the "form seemed to represent the desires of people to resonate with God. Music from around the world has the capacity to heal."[21]

So who cares about water reflecting our thoughts? Well, guess what mostly comprises that beefcake chassis of yours? Our hot bods are approximately 70 percent water. The hidden messages in water show us that our thoughts—which are vibration—are a "carrier wave of consciousness."[22]

The importance of the relationship between water and music to the physical body is evident in this text from *Loving Mozart.*

> The purpose of these sounds is multi-dimensional, extremely complex, and above all, healing.... The earthly body is mostly water. In this sense the body acts as a conductor, resonating to vibrations made around it. The sounds trigger, in the human form, a profound awareness and response on the cellular level.... One does not need to appreciate, or even pay attention, to this music to be healed by it. It plays on our minds and bodies like a beautiful light.... The conscious understanding responds with acknowledgement, and then with joy.[23]

Now, I gotta ask, seeing that H_2O comprises a significant part of our *hu*-man body, "What's up with **hu**?"

The word "hu" (pronounced you) is a direct reference to the Word of God in the ancient Sanskrit language. *Mana* in Sanskrit means "mind of the ordinary man." When we say or write the word *human*, we are implying that God and man are one and the same. We are hu-man, or God-man, or Goddess-wo-man to be politically correct.

I came across this *hu*-man connection years ago in a long forgotten text. It tickled my tongue that the word *hum* is part of human. Try humming for a moment. Hear that reverberation in your skull? The *sound* has nowhere else to go but *inside* of you. Or should I say *hu*? The words human, hum, and hu symbolize sound acting as a connector between our physical state and God.

When I *hum* with the specific intention of gaining greater self-awareness, am I trying to reactivate something *within* that is conscious of my own divinity? And wouldn't *hu* know it, on a recent TBIF CD the final song is all about humming.

Humming right along, if being *hu*-man means I am both a person and God simultaneously, perhaps music can act as a bridge for us poor souls, who as *hu*-mans have forgotten our *hu* for the most part? Can rock music help us to understand the divine mysteries and to express gratitude to God, or initiate our soul into its higher destiny—being *hu*-man? Dr. Emoto and the author of *Loving Mozart* claim that music can be healing. Maybe gospel or classical music, but rock 'n' roll? It seemed unlikely to me, but I was about to find out the answer is YES!

Had anyone in TBIF surmised the connection between sound, music, and healing? Why did their *sound* resonate so deeply within me?

The Law of Attraction states that like resonates with like. Yet I had to wonder, was there some kind of cosmic screw-up occurring between my soul and the souls of TBIF? I looked at a photo of the band and shook my head. They couldn't possibly have the slightest notion about the spiritual power of music.

I must be attracted to the wrong group. Why wasn't I drawn to U2, The Grateful Dead, Pink Floyd, or Yes?

One night, I pulled out all of TBIF's old albums from the basement closet. A particular sleeve engrossed me, because fans on the band's **message boards** had mentioned that various song titles and lyrics were depicted in photographed mini-scenes. I stared at several images, making a few connections to the lyrics when—WHAM!—I saw an incredible paragraph written on the upper left-hand corner of the sleeve that I had never paid attention to before. Where did this come from? I'd read this numerous times in 1980 when the album was first released, and had absolutely no conscious recollection of it. Alzheimer's must be accelerated by loud music.

I'm paraphrasing here, but the paragraph says that they hoped to live longer and triumph over physical decline due to the *healing force of music*. Without their vinyl records, they felt like crap; but when the music returned, life was great again. Not only that, they believed music was an addiction as well.

Wow. Thank you, merciful God, for answering my searing question. What were the odds that someone in the band would write this, only for me to discover it twenty-three years later when asking myself if anyone in the band understood the healing power of sound?

I later discovered that the words to the paragraph are actually in a song on the album. I recently listened again. Sure enough, the entire phrase is quickly spoken, and it's difficult to distinguish the words because the music is playing loudly over the guy's speech. It sounds like a HIDDEN message!

Is the healing force of music one of those hidden messages the intuitive Jalynn said were coming from TBIF's music? Maybe. Once-upon-a-time Beatles producer George Martin said, "They're a healing force in music." Can you guess which band he was he talking about? No, not the Fab Four—but another well-known quartet. Yeah. It was TBIF.

So let's connect all of the dots. Group reincarnation stories focus on past-life trauma. Did my soul group—TBIF and some of their fans—experience a traumatic previous lifetime together? If so, since vibration powerfully impacts *hu*mans in our water-based bods, music (vibration) may help us heal our trauma. Therefore, what could be a better way for a traumatized soul group to find inner harmony than with a rock band that has been dubbed a healing force in music?

Maybe I'm naive, but it's so plain to see. The writing is on the wall. Rock music can heal our body, mind, and soul.

CHAPTER 9

"GOOD VIBRATIONS"

—The Beach Boys

"The purpose of all Toning is to restore the vibratory pattern of the body to its perfect electro-magnetic field, so that it will function in harmony with itself."[24]

—Laurel Elizabeth Keyes, author, sound healer, spiritual teacher

Shortly after I awakened to the impact of music and sound upon the human psyche and body, an acquaintance asked if I'd heard of Jonathan Goldman, creator of the award-winning *Chakra Chants* CD and author of the classic sound-healing text *Healing Sounds*. No, I hadn't, but he *sounded* intriguing.

Through his website, I learned that Jonathan's theories dovetail nicely with my own. He offers a home-study correspondence class in using the voice to create vowel sounds as **mantras**. Sounded scrump-deli-icious! Sign me up! Over the next several months, I started making noises you wouldn't catch me doing anywhere but in the privacy of my walk-in closet.

How do you create a vowel sound and use it as a mantra? It's not as complex as you'd think. Whenever any sound is made, it creates a harmonic, or overtone. If you hit middle C on the piano, the C note is called the *fundamental* tone. But you also hear numerous other vibrations, which gives "C" or any other note a rich and complex sound. These are the *overtones*. Vocalizations create overtones as well, and it is overtones that allow us to have distinct, unique voices.

At the crux of Jonathan Goldman's sound-healing theories is a belief that overtones influence spiritual consciousness and physical well-being. "Meditation is a wonderful tool for enhanced relaxation and reduction of stress," he wrote. "Making sounds, particularly those which focus upon harmonics, is a very simple and easy way of achieving the same result. By producing long, drawn-out sounds, we are breathing more slowly and reducing our heart rate and brain waves as well. Creating vocal harmonics by itself becomes a form of meditation."[25]

As I considered myself a psychic brick and would rather give birth to a baby rhinoceros than meditate, I sincerely hoped that Jonathan's vocal exercises could open me to greater self-awareness.

Remember the seven chakras discussed earlier? Another perk of practicing the mantras is that the seven vowel sounds (uh, ooo, oh, ah, eye, aye, eee) can stimulate the corresponding seven chakra energy centers in the body. Not only that, overtones may open the **third eye** (also known as the sixth chakra) and enhance intuitive abilities, a way cool side-effect. So, naturally, I practiced my combination of uhs, ohs, ahs, ayes, and eees in my closet as often as possible.

At times, I could actually feel the resonance of certain sounds and pitches in various parts of my body, such as in my foot or arm. But the grooviest part was trying to actually create harmonic overtones.

Try this yourself. Make a really high-pitched *eee*. Hear that buzzing sound?

Or, say a long nasally *nuuuurrrr*. The buzzing resonance is a rudimentary form of a harmonic overtone. What an incredible feeling to hear this supersonic sound coming out of your mouth.

Get Yer Ya-Ya's Out! It's time for some fun, cause with a little practice you, too, can sit in your closet and create mind-expanding harmonic overtones.

Why would harmonic overtones, sound, and music have such a powerful impact? I believe it's because sound is a carrier wave of consciousness; the essence of consciousness is vibration.

Various books, such as *The Secret Power of Music, The Mysticism of Sound and Music, The Music of Life, Traveling the Sacred Sound Current, Ears of the Angels,* and *The World is Sound: Nada Brahma,* essentially claim the same thing: all things are God; all things vibrate; anything that vibrates creates sound (though we don't audibly hear most vibrations).

Therefore, GOD IS SOUND and VIBRATION.

Sound encodes information. At the creation of the universe, God said the "Word," and what is a word but a thought transmitted through the vibration of the voice?

Jonathan Goldman writes in *Healing Sounds* that a person's intention plays a vital role when using the human voice in the healing process. He developed the following formula: FREQUENCY + INTENTION = HEALING. "It means that the intention of the person working with the sound is as important as the frequency...."[26]

Here is an additional formula of Jonathan's for the same principles of frequency and intention: VISUALIZATION + VOCALIZATION = MANIFESTATION. "This formula developed through examination of the creation myths from many different traditions. In many of these myths, the creator God would manifest the world and all of its objects through sound. This God would visualize or first think of the object to create, placing intention upon this, then the God would vocalize the sound for the object, creating its frequency, and bringing it into being."[27]

The second formula seems really familiar. Hey, it parallels the Law of Attraction's steps to creation: Visualize what you desire. Ask for it (using your voice, or your thoughts/vibration). Then allow the Universe to bring your manifestation to you.

It's fascinating how the two principles are so similar. Could they possibly represent some kind of universal law about how *hu*-mans create reality? It seemed like some kind of important association.

A year after my introduction to Jonathan Goldman's music, I attended one of his weekend workshops in Boulder and was exposed to a variety of healing techniques involving sound. For two days, we sixty participants toned, chanted, sang, and played with tuning forks and other vibratory instruments. (Think Tibetan singing bowls.)

In the week leading up to the seminar, my ego's shadow had projected all kinds of crapola at me regarding TBIF. Since the band had no idea I was on this journey, the fear of writing this book about my possible past lives with them gave me many a sleepless night. Thankfully, the intensive exposure to a variety of sound-healing therapies helped soothe my stressed nerves and led to true sound healing.

At the workshop, the beginning exercise required us to say our first name, a color, then a word that might help us to heal. I chose Laura, Yellow, and Trust. We were to envision the color and the word, then as a group sing the name in an upward scale of four tones. It was powerful to hear everyone sing my name—and trust that I'd get over my fear of rejection from TBIF and their fans.

By the weekend's conclusion, my body was pulsing with new-found resonances. But the workshop's final exercise left the biggest impression on me. We formed two circles around a person who stated his or her name, a color, and what s/he wanted for healing. The group then sang that person's name over and over until it became a song. This continued for as long as it felt right, usually about five minutes.

The sound was reminiscent of an angelic choir. Each person who received the song said it powerfully impacted them both physically and emotionally. Some saw colors and felt energy surges and tingling. One person felt he'd entered an altered state of consciousness, and he cried tears of joy at the end of the song. Each participant felt they'd received whatever was necessary for their own healing.

Here's a little synchronicity for you. Even as a member of the chorus, I received a healing message too. The first person had the same name as the lead singer of TBIF. When I sang the name, it fused a strong energetic connection between me and the guy in the circle, as well as with the singer in the band.

The next person stated her intention, and the key word we visualized was *surrender*. That reminded me of a tune from TBIF. After we did our angel song, a woman in front of me turned and said, "You have a beautiful voice."

Laura, the dying wildebeest, has a nice voice? Really?

This woman's message was more than a nice compliment. *The Celestine Prophecy* says that everyone we meet has a message for us, and messages sometimes come in threes. The singer's name was number one. *Surrender* was two. "You have a beautiful voice" was three.

The three messages create the parts of the formula: VISU-ALIZATION + VOCALIZATION = MANIFESTATION. As I visualized and vocalized the image of the singer and the process of *surrender*, the manifestation was a proclamation that I have a beautiful voice. Was the Universe trying to let me know that *my* voice, and what I have to say, and write, is as beautiful and impor-tant as anyone else's?

After weeks of searching, humming, and chanting, this was definitely a message with which I could resonate. Surrender my fears and let the entire process unfold. Time to trust that my soul would show me everything I needed to write a book about group reincarnation and the healing power of music.

Easier said than done.

CHAPTER 10

"MAGIC MAN"

—Heart

"When I'm onstage, I feel this incredible, almost spiritual experience. Those great rock 'n' roll experiences are getting harder and harder to come by, because they have to transcend a lot of drug-induced stupor. But when they occur, they are sacred."[28]

—Pete Townshend, musician

My father always told me I do things backwards. Most people write a book after reflecting upon a jaw-dropping experience. I was penning my opus while the adventure was still unfolding. I tend to do things the hard way.

After researching group reincarnation, rereading between-life studies, and exploring the healing power of sound, my psychic compass slammed into a brick wall.

What's next? How will I write a book about reincarnation and rock music when I'm not an expert or intuitive? Think, think, think.

The library? Why not?

I scoured the metaphysical section and voila, a book on the bottom shelf screamed for attention: "LOOK AT ME, DOWN HERE!"

"What? No way. I'm not picking you up, you Tarot-card book you. You're associated with the occult and the dark arts. I don't do darkness."

But surprisingly, the Tarot book captivated me that day. So, I took it home.

I gotta admit, that book sat on my table all lonely for a week or two. It still kinda weirded me out—evoking images of fortune-tellers, gypsies, Miss Cleo, and the Psychic Friends Network. But I learned you can't always judge a card by its picture.

After several weeks, the library book grew impatient. "Open me!!" it squawked. All right, already. I peeled open the tome and saw lots and lots of pictures. A few images looked somewhat disturbing, but overall the cards weren't scary at all. Maybe this was just what this *psychic brick* needed on her journey to greater self-discovery?

Over the next few weeks, I learned that the **Tarot** is actually a spiritual tool. It provides deeper insights for those willing to look inside themselves. How? The images reflect an "archetype" of human experience.

ARCHETYPE? Was this some kind of twisted cosmic ha-ha? The word "archetype" had been camping out in my brain with lawn chairs...and here was a spiritual tool that focused on it! Thanks, Law of Attraction! Psychic compass is A-OK.

The Tarot book got me psyched enough to buy my own deck of Tarot cards. But which kind? I started with the best-selling **Universal Waite** deck, created in 1909 by mystic Arthur Edward Waite.

Then I checked out the popular **Thoth** Tarot deck by Aleister Crowley. There's all kind of controversy around Crowley, but I revived him from the dead because he crops up a lot in rock 'n' roll circles. There's Ozzy Osborne's song "Mr. Crowley." Did you know Mr. Jimmy Page of Led Zeppelin bought Crowley's castle? And Crowely was so popular, The Beatles included him on the "people we like" cover of *Sgt. Pepper's Lonely Hearts Club Band* (second person from the left, top row). So Hi-Ho, Hi-Ho, it's off to study the Tarot I go!

Though there are hundreds of decks with various themes,

they all contain a Major and Minor Arcana (the word *arcanum* means "secret knowledge"). The **Major Arcana** consists of 22 cards, each numbered 0 to 21, symbolizing our physical, intellectual, emotional, and spiritual aspects. The **Minor Arcana** is comprised of 56 cards in four different suits. The Major Arcana expresses universal themes; the Minor Arcana puts those themes into practical use and represents the concerns, activities, and emotions that make up our everyday lives.

All Tarot decks work with the same *archetypes* (e.g., The Magician, The Emperor, The Lovers). Most importantly, the Tarot cards symbolize the path of the mythic hero's journey to self-realization. And who is the Hero? That would be you and me: all human beings. In the Tarot, the hero is symbolized by the first card of the Major Arcana, #0, The Fool.

The Fool (me) is on the Rock 'n' Roll Yellow Brick Road of self-discovery, and the Tarot became my trusty side-kick. What better tool could a psychic brick ask for? And it has pictures! I don't sense energy, see auras, or hear dead people. So the Tarot cards became my perfect muse to trust my intuition and inner guidance on my odyssey.

After working with the Tarot for a surprisingly short time, I couldn't help but notice how familiar the cards felt, as though something long forgotten was once again revealing itself. Often, I *knew* the overall meanings of the symbols without even reading about them.

That's the beauty of archetypes. They're imprinted on our psyche—but lie dormant until we **Wake the Bleep Up** to them! This made my heart go pitter-patter. I had finally found my true metaphysical "home."

That feeling of "home" often manifests as a tingly sensation in the body, when your soul offers a heads-up that something important had just made its way into your cerebellum. When I read the following sentence in Jonathan Goldman's *Healing Sounds*: "In the Ancient Mystery Schools, the priests and magicians were often also the musicians,"[29] a tingling sensation engulfed dense little ol' me. **Priests, Magicians, Musicians?** Verrry interesting.

Many Tarot books acknowledge that the Ancient Mystery Schools highly influenced the imagery in the Tarot archetypes. The first numbered card in the Major Arcana (#1) is The Magician, and the fifth card is the High Priest (a.k.a. Pope or Heirophant). I had discovered a sentence about Priests, Magicians, and Musicians in a book on sound healing, and priests and magicians are also in the Tarot. An important connection? Neato!

But what are the Ancient Mystery Schools? In Greece and Egypt, they were centers of study and mystic initiation that educated students on natural laws and principles, and encouraged introspection in order to "know thyself." The meaning of the word *mystery* stems from the Greek *mysteria*, or "secret rite or doctrine"; and *mystes* "one who has been initiated." Through the Tarot and other clues that I was feeling prompted to follow, I was getting *initiated* into the Mystery School of Rock 'n' Roll.

Many current religions have descended from the Ancient Mystery Schools. The ancient teachings influenced the **Freemasons** and **Rosicrucians** as well as the spiritual society known as the **Hermetic Order of the Golden Dawn.** (Arthur Edward Waite, creator of the Universal Waite Tarot deck, and Aleister Crowley were members of the Golden Dawn).

As I waded through the Ancient Mystery School references in various texts, one word kept appearing in my research: **alchemy.** I vaguely remembered my high-school science teacher claiming that alchemy was the bling-bling rage during the Middle Ages and Renaissance, when dudes in dark robes tried to turn base metals such as lead into gold.

I've since discovered that my teacher knew only half the story. Yes, attempts to transform crappy metals into gold did take place, and those alchemists are often credited with being the forerunners to today's chemists. But the Tarot, especially the Universal Waite deck, opened my eyes to the true power of alchemy. Alchemy was not simply about physical change—but spiritual transformation. Alchemists developed a process for *humans* to transform to a higher spiritual understanding through esoteric symbols and images.

Let's go back to "the priests and magicians were often also the musicians." Focus on the word *magician*. Nowadays, we think of magicians as Houdini, Penn & Teller, or Criss Angel doing their tricks of illusion, but guess what I found out? During the Middle Ages, the terms alchemy and magic were frequently interchangeable, because they both sought to transform the physical into the spiritual. Alchemists = Magicians.

As with the word mystery, we've lost our connection to the real meaning of magic. The word magic stems from *magi*, meaning "learned and *priestly* class." Since magic and alchemy both focus on spiritual transformation, it would seem that in the past, magicians were truly priests. Magicians = Priests.

Magic has made a resurgence in our society with *Harry Potter*, but true *magic* is extremely misunderstood by us Muggles. How could someone wave a wand, say a few words, and put a curse on the nasty old lady next door, or help Aunt Betty relieve her boils? Preposterous, that's what I always thought. But as I explored more of the Ancient Mystery School teachings, it became apparent that magic has a very long history. Here's the skinny:

Alchemical *magic* attempts to weave two worlds together: the seen and the unseen. Most magicians believed that nothing can come into physical existence unless it first takes shape in the higher (or unseen) worlds. This is reflected by the ancient

Hermetic axiom that alchemists and magicians embraced: As above, so below.

So, what is the creative power behind magic? No, it isn't having a pretty crystal ball or a cool magic wand. It's a nifty three-parter: intention, emotion, and visualization.

Magicians during the Middle Ages trained their minds to hold a visualization of an object or an intention for a period of time. This is similar to "creative visualization" techniques, but must also be coupled with intention. The stronger our desire—or intention—the greater the energy instilled into what we want manifested.

As reviewed earlier, our intention and thoughts are vibration. Even Dr. Emoto's frozen crystals showed that the intention behind the words written on paper impacted the water crystals. However, sound—specifically the human voice—helps to augment our intention.

So, what would a smart magician do? Use her voice to amplify her intention! If you recall, Danae the intuitive saw a previous lifetime in which a member of TBIF and I had created physical emanations in the air with our voices. That sounds uncannily similar to the creation process used by ancient magicians. Just a coincidence, right?

The ancient magicians understood that a word—when spoken and felt with emotion—had great influence. It created a physical vibration, which carried their intention and in some way led to a manifestation in the world. According to the book *Hidden Wisdom*, "Though most magicians ascribe tremendous power to sacred words and names, this power does not lie so much in the word's meaning as in its emotional effect on the participants, and some say, in the very vibrations of the sounds."[30]

The ancient magicians used intention and vibration in a similar way as musicians—to cause an effect without physical interaction. Musicians permeate notes with their desire and intention in order to relay emotion to listeners: bloodcurdling, irate, jubilant, serene, etc. Magicians recite incantations with intention. Are you ready for the connection between musicians and magicians? *Both use sound as a carrier wave of intention and information.* How do ya' like them apples? Musicians = Magicians!

Everything discussed mirrors the Law of Attraction and Jonathan Goldman's formulas: Frequency + Intention = Healing; and Visualization + Vocalization = Manifestation; which circles back to the creation myths in which God had an intention, spoke the Word, and physical matter came into being. If the word *hu*man is indicative of man simultaneously being God-like, perhaps it is also a sign that we are truly magicians and co-creators with this Universal Consciousness.

I later stumbled upon numerous other texts and websites that had culled quotes from many iconic contemporary rock musicians—including Keith Richards, John Lennon, and Pete Townshend—stating that they feel like shamans, mediums, or channels when creating and performing music. Many rock legends refer to the *magic* experienced on stage with a live audience. Jimi Hendrix took this concept even further when he said, "Rock music is more than music, IT'S LIKE CHURCH." Are rock musicians modern-day High Priests of rhythmic noise? Priests = Magicians = Musicians!

I might be just a Fool on this archetypal journey toward self-discovery—but Fools aren't stupid. We're open to all kinds of possibilities, and that includes the possibility that magic exists.

CHAPTER 11
"WITH A LITTLE HELP FROM MY FRIENDS"

—The Beatles

"Rock's noise has been necessary to break through the crust of self-consciousness accumulated over these last three thousand years. So that a place long asleep in us would wake. In the instant environment of rock, the literally deafening noise cancels out the rest of the culture."[31]

—Michael Ventura, novelist, essayist, and cultural critic

One night, shortly after the Tarot and magic stuff had entered my consciousness, an unusual dream skied through my delta brainwaves.

I was in a store and saw a pile of earrings on a table. Next to the earrings were octopus necklaces. An older woman came over and said her name was Candy and that it was a good foundation for a name. She mentioned that she had to lose a little more weight, but I told her she looked fine. I woke up wondering what important pearl of wisdom my subconscious wanted me to glean from this odd dream. Earrings pointed to the ear…and hearing. Perhaps something to do with sound?

A dream interpretation website defines earrings as suggestive of encouraging and interesting work to do and a possible meaning of the word *jewelry*—"signifying value in the spiritual sense of protection." So did I need spiritual protection while writing my book? But Candy as a foundation for a name stumped me. Were we talking M&M's, or what???

Then this thought popped into my cranium: *Earrings (ears) have to do with listening.* The prefix of octopus, *oct*, is the beginning of *octave*—another reference to sound. A name that *sounds* like Candy? Oh, my heavens! TBIF's deceased merchandise manager's last name started with the letters c-a-n-d or can-d! Since I'd had that paranormal experience with him (the loud popping noise in my bathroom with the brilliant blue light), this made sense. He had used *sound* to get my attention that night.

I turned to the Tarot for clarity about the dream. The cards indicated a new project coming into my life, and that its fulfillment would depend upon my spiritual awakening. I'd have to trust my intuition for things to unfold.

But what's this? The Emperor card? (see appendix for image) A leader or father figure? Holy guacamole, Batman! It's the merchandise man!

He had a beard and long white hair, just like the Emperor! Was his spirit trying to help me **Wake the Bleep Up?** Maybe I wasn't such a psychic brick after all! I'd asked the Universe to send me help, but I'd never imagined it might be the spirit of TBIF's deceased merchandise manager. Now I had an etheric friend to guide me. Instead of calling him Candyman, I used his initials JC.

Several weeks later, I studied the Tarot for insights as to what TBIF symbolized to their fans. The **spread** (card layout) indicated that they are messengers and visionary leaders, and the Tower card, specifically, signified that their music is intended to shake us awake.

"What does their music represent to us?" I asked JC and the Tarot cards.

Sexual energy, insight, intuition, inspiration, and joy, was the answer.

The music helps us get in touch with our inner wisdom. I nodded to myself. Of course. TBIF was a catalyst for change…through their music.

A week later, I asked the Tarot about my soul connection with TBIF. Several cards got my attention. The Judgment card revealed an awakening of a group of people. **Wake the Bleep Up!**

Next was the Page of Swords. Was that ME? A messenger of truth? I was to cut through the illusions…and deliver a message to humanity? No way! You're freakin' me out! Would somebody please shove my head in a toilet and snap me back to reality?

Then the 10 of Pentacles, which usually represents success and abundance, caught my attention. I looked at that card for several minutes. Suddenly, I noticed a black-and-white checkerboard pattern inconspicuously going down the side of the card.

What's that for? It has nothing to do with the other images.

Suddenly, a metaphysical two-by-four whacked me in the forehead. My heart raced. The earth shook. Drum roll please: *the alternating black-and-white squares of a checkerboard—a major symbol in ancient alchemy and magic—represent the duality of consciousness and unconsciousness, good and evil.* I couldn't believe it! It's TBIF's MOTIF. The image on their albums and guitars was an alchemical symbol? Holy crap.

Finally! A missing piece of the puzzle that linked many seemingly unrelated themes. Musicians = Magicians!

After my heart palpitations subsided, I asked the Tarot to tell me about the band's energy in a past life. As I shuffled, The Magician card literally flew out of the deck. And I didn't even say Abracadabra! What a coincidence.

Come to think of it, the band's name implies light-hearted deception, or a slight of hand as in *magic*; and the Magician card represents the Trickster archetype in mythology. HA! In my mind, this was a neon-chaser light clue!

Life is not just black and white (squares). It's a kaleidoscope. Looking through my scope, I saw not only an amazing array of colors and geometrical shapes, but some letters. What did they spell? "G-E-T O-U-T O-F D-E-N-V-E-R, B-A-B-Y. G-O." Go where?

"Hotel California!"

CHAPTER 12

"RAY OF LIGHT"

— Madonna

"I've noticed that with a lot of people that urge to be creative…comes from a feeling of not belonging in this world, always feeling out of place."[32]
—Michael McDonald, musician

The ability to conjure a spell to draw TBIF back to Denver eluded me. It had been a year since I saw them in concert and withdrawal symptoms were starting to arise. The band had a few dates scheduled in California and several of my friends lived in the vicinity of the shows. *Me thinks a trip to Los Angeles is a splendid idea.* But there was another reason to go to the concerts besides getting my music fix.

Back when the word *archetype* was constantly in my face after my awakening, I had asked the intuitive Lee what the hell this had to do with rock music. Her guidance suggested that I poll fans to discover what archetype their favorite band represented to them. *What? Most fans wouldn't know an archetype from the Arch de Triumph.*

Instead of archetypes, could I ask what myth or fairy tale a band represented to the fans? I wondered. But how? It was an unusual question. *Think, think, think.*

Well, I was a radio marketing-research analyst, so why not write a rock-music survey? I could ask fans all kinds of music-related questions and use the data for my book. Voila! But the idea made my stomach twist into a funky knot. Putting a survey out into the world would mean I was really writing a book…a book connecting group reincarnation and rock music. Gulp.

For ideas on how to approach the research, I checked out the only two books I could find about rock music fans: *Tramps Like Us* (Bruce Springsteen fans) and *In the Houses of the Holy* (Led Zeppelin fans). Both included fan surveys, so several similar demographic-like questions made their way into my own questionnaire. However, mine also included queries like: "Ever recall dreams of your favorite band?"

Several days before flying off to California for two shows at the Anaheim House of Blues, I posted on the band's message board whether anyone was interested in filling out my survey. Only one brave soul said he'd talk about his fandom. Well, it was a start.

The night before my trip, I consulted the Tarot (and JC) about attending the concerts. The overall theme answered in the cards was sadness and fear. This totally surprised me, because I was stoked to see the band again.

I then asked what made me afraid, and, when I turned the cards over, the Magician (the card that symbolized TBIF to me) was surrounded by cards of fear and emotional upset. *What??* I was afraid of magic?

Usually the meanings of the cards immediately jumped out and kissed me, but this time I felt no definite answers, and my pace of understanding was as slow as a sea slug. But I hoped that eventually a deeper meaning would be revealed.

I arrived later than expected at the House of Blues—and felt incredibly dorky handing out my survey—so I changed my game plan. Instead, I occasionally tossed out a question while waiting in line, such as: "What other rock bands were you into as a teenager?" The answers? Mostly the same groups I had been into because the majority of people I spoke to were close to my own age…old as dirt!

Once inside the general-admission theater, I snagged my usual spot, a few rows back on the guitarist's side of the stage. The show was extremely high energy, some celebrities were in the audience, and everyone was having a blast.

After my concert high, it was difficult to sleep, but golden slumber finally overcame my exhausted body. The next morning, I sat on my hotel-room bed and, and, to my surprise, tears streamed down my face. I was wallowing in the Boo-Hoo Blues. Where on earth was this coming from? It didn't make sense.

Then I recalled that after seeing the band perform years ago in 1998 in Seattle, an intense blanket of despair had overwhelmed me then, too. Also, for no apparent reason. *Why, why, why did seeing the band make me cry, cry, cry?* What the bleep was WRONG with me?

I didn't want to admit it, but lots of fans were getting attention from the band. Yet none of the guys seemed to recognize *me* in the audience. In fact, whenever one band member looked my way, he appeared to get a twinge of mistrust in his eyes, and would quickly look away from me. Now that I think about it, he'd done that during the Colorado Springs concert two years earlier.

Oh, right. I sobbed after that concert, too.

Gawk Girl can't make eye contact with anyone in the band. So, I'm getting my own crap reflected back at me? Is this the Law of Attraction at work?

Before I had left home for the California concerts, the Tarot had predicted sadness would be a major theme for me. Fortunately, I brought my deck with me, so I turned to the cards (and JC) again for guidance.

"Why did this concert dig up such intense feelings of grief?" I asked.

The cards reflected my current emotional state, and showed

a tremendous sorrow about a past situation. The 5 of Pentacles indicated feeling rejected by being excluded from a group. An important clue!

I arrived at the House of Blues about four in the afternoon, planning to interview fans who had also arrived stupid early, but I got a vibe that some folks weren't receptive to my presence. Maybe because I was an ultra-nerdy singleton (a woeful fan who attends a concert alone). Then something weird kicked in. I couldn't stop worrying about what everyone else was thinking about me.

The Tarot cards were right on target and my ego snickered, *Don't introduce yourself to anyone. They probably won't like you.*

This, of course, spawned more insecurity, and for some reason, I felt more gigantic than usual. Tall dumb blond, is that how they saw me?

Probably not. But all I could think was *I'm a Super Freak with a dorky black sparkly hat!* Not only was I physically different, but mentally too. It felt as though Gawk Girl was the only fan in the universe interested in spirituality and rock music. I put so much pressure on myself seeking insights for the book that I wasn't being real. So once again, I ditched the idea of trying to interview anyone for the survey.

While standing in line, I simply watched the fans interact with one another. Mega rays of light. Smiles. Lots of smiles. Peals of laughter. Shrieks of joy. "Oh, my God! I haven't seen you in for-eeeh-ver. Isn't it wonderful that the band brings us together?"

Music makes it easier for everyone to sparkle. Fans sing and dance, without a care of what they look like. My light could shine just as brilliantly, I muttered to myself, if I would allow it! When a woman is confident in herself, she shines brightly to all. When self-esteem lags, we sometimes attempt to snuff-out another person's light.

I remembered one night after a different TBIF show, when three inebriated women were staggering toward their car. One yelled at the top of her lungs, "Oh, my GAWD! Did you see how HOT the singer's ass looked in those pants?" That certainly got my attention.

Then they spotted another woman walking ahead wearing the exact same black high-heeled boots as the yeller, and both women were wearing skirts to show off their legs. A friend in the threesome screamed that *her* buddy's boots looked *soooo* much better than on the other chick. Then the third friend piped up and trashed the boot-clone, too. Claws emerged. A cat fight was about to ensue. Fortunately, boot-clone ignored them and I didn't have to play referee. I shook my head. *Both* women were attractive in their boots. Jealousy didn't enhance anyone's light. It only choked their brilliance.

Yet, like the insecure women, Invisible Girl felt pangs of jealousy tonight around these other fans. Outsider in so many ways.

That was until I entered the theater when a sign from the Universe was handed to me. As I stood waiting for the warm-up band, I felt an intuitive nudge. *UP HERE! Look at me!*

Way up toward the ceiling, the words "Unity Through Diversity" were emblazoned across the wall, along with several spiritual icons, including a yin/yang symbol and an Eastern religious statue.

I pondered my illusion of being alienated and alone. Unity Through Diversity. That was how I felt during the magic of a concert. The symbols shifted my perspective…and my attitude.

Then two women from the Los Angeles all-female tribute band Cheap Chick moseyed up to me and had me in stitches with their hilarious stories about being female rockers. Out of the blue, the bassist and founder, Pam, invited me to join their band.

I laughed so hard, the water I was drinking came out my

nose. "I lack one important thing: talent."

Oh, and I live a thousand miles away. Thanks, but no thanks. You rock on, girlfriends. My electric guitar and French horn days are long behind me. I'll sit at a computer and write a book instead.

But I grinned. Thanks for thinking that Gawk Girl could possibly be included in your band. Maybe my ideas of separation from other fans *were* just figments of my imagination, after all.

PART TWO

"Time Travel Fantasy"
—Jackson Browne

"Friends are all souls that we've known in other lives. We're drawn to each other. Even if I have only known them a day, it doesn't matter. I'm not going to wait till I have known them for two years, because anyway, we must have met somewhere before, you know." —George Harrison

CHAPTER 13

"PEOPLE ARE STRANGE"

—The Doors

"My discussion with Keith Richards about the creative process led me to believe that there's an invisible presence of a stream of ever-flowing creativity that we overhear—all you have to do is pull up the antenna and dial it." [33]

—Billy F. Gibbons, musician

Two days after 2003's New Year, an intuitive tingling nudged me to dredge up an old TBIF piano book and reread the lyrics to an unusual song. The tune contained a verse of ambiguous lyrics that made not one iota of sense...but it included the word Colorado, my favorite state. Since I'm not using actual song titles here, I'll refer to it as the "Colorado" song, not to be confused with the other Colorado song, John Denver's "Rocky Mountain High."

Anyway, the tune focuses on a guy warning a girl to look out for some dude who wants to get her. Then the lyrics launch into Strangeville. Because I was residing in Strangeville myself, it seemed that something significant was hidden in the lyrics, especially the lines about looking for riddles and clues, a woman going to a river, and three (as in 3) saying to look out in the directions of south and east. The second to last line of the verse says not to go to Colorado, and the word "march" evokes images of soldiers marching, at least in my mind, for some Strangeville reason.

I consulted the Tarot and asked what the bizarre stanza

meant for *me*. The 3 of Wands (see appendix for Tarot images) stood out since it also eerily matched TBIF's motif and song lyrics. It included a man in a cloak with a *checkerboard* stripe, *looking out* over a *river* with *three* ships sailing on the water. (Wands symbolize the compass point *south*.)

It sounds crazy, but the other cards, including the Lovers (symbolizing the attraction between a guy and girl) and 7 of Swords (means being sneaky), also seemed to tell a story that synched with the lyrics. Was it a coincidence? I wasn't sure.

Perhaps TBIF's guitarist, who wrote the lyrics, was tapped into the collective unconscious? The number three, a river, and other elements of the verse *were* fairly universal symbols. The cards were certainly helping *me* tap into *my* collective unconscious. This Tarot spread gave me more confidence that I (under the guidance of my soul) was on the right track as a rock 'n' roll reincarnation sleuth.

Not long after New Year's, I heard that TBIF was going to perform some shows in the northwest during the month of March. Several of my husband's relatives lived in cities where the band was scheduled to play, so I decided to take my young daughters to see family while I hit a few concerts.

A show in Boulder, Colorado was later added to TBIF's tour for the beginning of April. I got a fantabulous idea! What if several local intuitives went to the concert and gave me their psychic impressions of the band, music, and the fans? As a former radio marketing-research analyst, I craved unbiased perspectives. But now my laboratory would be an exciting rock concert, instead of ho-hum boring numbers and statistics.

I attended a local St. Patty's Metaphysical Celebration in the hope of meeting some new psychics with whom I had no prior connection. The event was unlike any other I had ever attended. Lots of Tarot, astrology, and numerology readers. Tons of clairvoyants. Several handwriting, palmistry, reiki, missing persons, and past-life readers. If you were a skeptic and walked into that room, a neon sign would shriek, "Run for your life!" *New Age* reeked from every booth, practitioner, and participant. Esoteric vibes permeated the very air. I was in Nirvana.

Charol, a clairvoyant and writer, saw a past-life connection between the band and me without knowing their name.

"I'm getting images of traveling minstrels, troubadours. I don't know modern music that much, but when I see the group, on a spiritual level they are operating on a higher octave. If you took a scale, it's like up here."

"I'm assuming there are three or four fellows, and I'm getting that there is a group karma thing. It feels like play. In fact, the whole sense of it just feels like children playing."

"I think there have been many connections with you and the band, and you all play many roles at different times. I get this giddy child-like energy that is bubbly and having fun. The connection for you now is that you are all operating on a higher octave, and the work you are doing and the work they are doing, is not necessarily together, but you are both putting out something with a similar vibe on this higher octave."

Wow. If Charol was accurate, then maybe on some level TBIF was aware of their music's influence beyond simple entertainment.

Just before leaving the fair, two women named Heidi and Rebecca overheard me ask the director of a psychic organization if she knew of any intuitives who might want to participate in my concert experiment. Both ladies said my concept of group reincarnation among rock fans sounded interesting and they'd be happy to attend the show and give me feedback. I hadn't intended to make this an "all chick challenge" for there are many excellent male psychics. Nevertheless, the Universe had brought me the intuitives I'd asked for.

But first there were four other shows in the Northwest: two in the Seattle area, the other two in Eugene and Portland, Oregon. I got to put on my Superfan sparkly hat and invisible cape again!

The previous shows in California had made it clear that I needed a better avenue to survey fans. I'd decided on the Internet. For the northwest shows, my website was up, my fan survey was ready to roll, and all I had to do was hand out business cards with two web addresses: one for TBIF fans, one for the fans of other bands. Folks could respond at home if they wanted to participate, and I didn't have to lug a briefcase to a rock concert.

Despite my optimism, my commitment to publishing a book about rock fans *and* group reincarnation had not yet hit 100 percent. What if I gave out the cards and no one responded to my survey? What exactly was the overall *bleeping* point of the book anyway? Patience little Grasshopper. Patience.

Two handfuls of TBIF's newsgroup fans met for dinner before the first show in Tacoma, Washington. Several people asked me if I had been at the Three Night Stand concerts in Seattle five years before. My food nearly adorned my lap.

"Holy hole in the donut, Batman, you remember me?" (Robin, the Boy Wonder, really did say the "donut" part.)

Maybe my sparkly hat had prompted their recollection, but the feeling of connection felt great. I definitely was supposed to be at this dinner because I met a woman I nicknamed **Sundante**. She later became an important player in my rock music/past-life odyssey.

The band put on a good performance in Tacoma, but I was in the second row, and way over on the left side of the stage by several massive speakers. All hail ear plugs! I could barely see the bassist on the other side of the stage and didn't feel connected with the band. No boo-hoos. Just wanted to get closer at the next show.

Two evenings later, I sloshed my rental car through a heavy downpour to the Eugene, Oregon concert. During the rainy ride, a peculiar memory of a college dance with my then-boyfriend (who would become my husband despite the upcoming remark) surfaced from the depths of my ROM (computer geek talk for Read Only Memory). It was during the big hair 1980s and I was doing some fancy footwork, which I thought made me look fantabulous.

However, my beau guffawed, "You dance like Buddy Ebsen!"

"Buddy Ebsen? Jed Clampett in *The Beverly Hillbillies?* The old geezer on *Barnaby Jones?*"

Well, he *had* been a vaudeville dancer in his youth. However, being compared to an outdated octogenarian was never erased from my databank. After that evening, I was squeamish even thinking about moving my size 27 shoes more than two millimeters in a crowded room.

Why did that memory pop up now? I wondered.

Still driving in the rain, I visualized my chakras glowing and spinning with their respective colors, and I repeated a **mantra:** "Slow down. Be present. Remain grounded."

The energy from concert music had always shot out the top of my head and I found it difficult to stay **grounded**. Tonight, I needed to be present and not drift off into an alternate dimension of musical bliss.

Not only that, but the ear-splitting vibrations (even with earplugs) always created a funky time warp. An hour felt like the blink of my third eye. I hate that! The concert is over when it feels like it just started.

I wanted to savor every moment this time. I also sensed something important might happen. Before finding a parking space, I set the intention to get up close to the band.

Under the cold drenching rain, I sprinted to the concert

hall. Yikes! Double-packed. My heart sank. None of the first few rows had any openings.

I headed to a side aisle, and heard a familiar voice call my name. I pirouetted and there was Sundante waving at me. She and her friend had snagged first-row seats and saved an extra spot.

"I don't know why I saved an extra seat," she said. "I just did."

Skippy yippy! Set that intention and watch the wonders of the Law of Attraction at work.

But when the guys came out on stage, it suddenly dawned on me: I was only two feet away from them. I'd never been this close before. Oh, crap. No one to block Gawk Girl from the band.

Front row sounds awesome, but I actually felt uncomfortably exposed. One of the guys had a perplexed look on his face when he saw me—towering above the women around me, a Sequoia in a grove of Bonsai trees. Every cell in my body squawked, *Sit Down!*

Sit? I trusted that my soul had landed me in the front row for a good reason. Besides, sitting down was the whimpola option. So I stood my ground amidst all the Bonsai fans.

Well, well, well. Tonight the guitarist noticed me. True, it was hard *not* to notice Miss Sequoia in the sparkly hat…but he interacted with me from the stage with gestures, as he always did with fans in the audience. I couldn't believe it. He actually saw me. ME! Invisible Gawk Girl!

I parroted back his gestures, and my face hurt from smiling so much. Every now and then, I'd think of something spiritual, then get swept away by the music, with wondrous energy coursing through my body. Maybe doing those chakra exercises had helped me maintain my balance to a degree?

Then it happened. My eyes were sorta closed. My body was swaying to the music. When I looked up at one point, the guitarist was making fun of how I moved, teasing me in a light-hearted way. But it immediately triggered my Buddy Ebsen complex. I was mortified. Did someone say "spaz?" Oh, for the love of God.

I made a complete fool of myself, but I couldn't help it. That's what their music does to me!

I took the teasing personally at first. My initial impulse was to retreat into my old pattern and sit down. Yet I didn't want to run away from discomfort anymore. I decided to face this uncomfortable moment and be present in it, to grow beyond my fear.

After a few minutes, I forced myself to make eye contact with the guitarist again briefly. It felt intimate...and a bit awkward at the same time, but I didn't die! I may have looked like a gawk, yet it wasn't the end of the world. So what if he goofed on me? He often has fun with fans in the front rows, especially those that he recognizes. That was part of the reason fans loved to watch him. He wasn't only a great musician, he interacts with the audience. We matter to him.

Now there was no doubt in my mind that after forty some-odd TBIF concerts, the guitarist recognized me. He might not know my name, but he wouldn't forget the tall Sequoia with the sparkly hat who moved like Buddy Ebsen.

My weird push-pull fear-attraction thingy with the band and fans would keep getting triggered at upcoming concerts, and ultimately, more of my funky fears would swell up from the depths of my unconscious as I skipped on down the Rock 'n' Roll Yellow Brick Road.

CHAPTER 14

"ME AND MY SHADOW"

—Al Jolson and Dave Dreyer, lyrics by Billy Rose

"When writing, you have to plumb into the subconscious, and there's a lot of scary things down there…you come back with a lot of self-knowledge, which then gives you greater human knowledge, and that helps. To know yourself is to know the world…. So in that way, the writing process is fantastic psychotherapy—if you can survive. But it is tricky."[34]

—Joni Mitchell, musician

Oftentimes, days or weeks after a concert, powerful insights come my way. This time, I realized…the band was becoming my therapist. I was starting to see hidden parts of myself that needed healing. I still felt awkward around the guys…and panicked at the idea of having to one day tell them I was writing a book about reincarnation and *our* possible past lives together. Ugh. Twisty, knotty stomach pains again.

Despite my phobia of looking like a spaz, the guitarist had given me exactly what I longed for: his attention. Most of us believe that outside factors can render us powerful, sexy, or smart. A nice car, a pretty wife, or a rock star smiling at us provides a good ego jolt. He certainly boosted mine.

Yet what happens if we haven't developed a sense of self, independent of appearances? What happens after our face has wrinkled like Yoda, our derrier tattoos have stretched, and gravity has wrought havoc on our various physical assets? If we focus only on the physical aspect of our being, we miss a huge opportunity to discover our spiritual "hu" beauty of being truly *hu*-man.

The process of simply accepting *who* we are at all times, no matter who we are with or what we look like, is referred to as **self-actualization**. Starting this quest isn't usually something we wake up to one morning and add to our "to-do list." *Note to self: Get to know my inner being today.* For me, it's been a gradual process of inward examination integrated into my daily life.

So, how do we commence consciously on the path to self-actualization? First, it helps to understand the underlying perspective of our **ego**. One interpretation is that the ego is the mental image of ourselves that develops as we grow up. It is the part of us that defines who we are through our interpretations of the past. Our ego believes its perspective is real, but it is not—because we are not really our past. We are whomever we choose to be in *this* moment. Sounds like a nice plan, but ain't gonna happen easily.

Ever wonder why certain painful life lessons are frequently repeated? Unlike Robert Palmer, who warned us that we're hopelessly addicted to love, (hit eighties tune, in case you forgot), the ego is usually addicted to *pain*. Eckhart Tolle, German spiritual teacher and author of *The Power of Now*, says we carry an accumulation of old emotional pain in our energy field. "It consists of negative emotions that were not faced, accepted, and then let go in the moment they arose."[35]

These emotions leave a residue, which is stored in the cells of the body and are referred to as the "pain body." This concept reflects my belief that the *water* in our body stores past memories and emotions, especially unhealed traumatic ones. I would eventually come to realize I had a "pain body" the size of Jupiter. And guess which rock band helped me heal the bugger?

I hate to break it to you, but every *hu*-man has an ego, and a nice archetypal sidekick called the shadow. They go together, like Jimmy Page and Robert Plant, or macaroni and cheese. I frequently refer to these psychological pain-in-the-butts as the **ego-shadow.** Our shadow represents the nasty, bad, ugly things we have repressed that we don't want anyone to see out of fear of rejection. Like my lovely dance moves.

Here's a rule of thumb: The higher the degree of irritation, fear, or upset, the more likely our ego-shadow is being triggered. Problem is, the ego believes *everyone else* is to blame when we feel like crap. *We* are never the problem. By understanding the concept of our ego-shadow, we can begin to see how we project our issues *onto* others. I was learning how I projected my issues onto TBIF.

Transference is when our feelings toward an individual are superimposed onto another. Something, perhaps the way the person looks or acts, reminds us subconsciously of the *original* person with whom we had the issue. My ego-shadow feared rejection from the band—but what was I transferring? I wondered. Could an unconscious memory from a past-life trigger my ego-shadow?

At this point, I was like Helen Keller, totally in the dark. The word *rejection* wasn't even part of my lexicon the night of my next concert in Boulder, Colorado.

The show was electrifying! My *laboratory* was brimming with rock fans. The psychics Heidi, Rebecca, and Anne were reading everyone's energy. The guitarist remembered me from several nights earlier in Oregon! That's power, baby! Shadow? What shadow? Each concert had provided insights, increasing my confidence about writing the book. I felt connected with everyone in the room. The concept that we are all energetically ONE was palpable. I could look the guitarist in the eye without turning into Troll Girl. Yay!!! Life was *bleeping* fantabulous. At least for a few days.

I shared this feeling of being powerful with my intuitive friend Anne, who had attended the concert. She was also getting her Master's degree in counseling. "Laura, you're not in your power," she corrected me. "You're still projecting and transferring your stuff onto the band. I could see it while I watched you."

I hate it when people get advanced degrees and become such smarty pants. Man, that totally took the wind out of my sails. You mean I'm not there yet? Time for a reality check.

I still couldn't see how my ego-shadow was playing tricks on me. You'd think my fear of rejection would have been blown to smithereens since the guitarist interacted with me again. He even threw me his bottled water at the end of the show. But no.

At last I saw that as long as the band was on stage, my ego-shadow was chilling out. I was safe out here in the audience. But when I thought about *speaking* to any of them about this book I was writing, a twisty knot in my stomach made me want to vomit.

The teacher Abraham has said, "You are eternal beings. You will never ever get it done, and you'll never get it wrong." I hate it when dead spirits say crap like that. Never get it done? Then why bother doing it at all? I guess it's because the joy is in the journey.

Despite Abraham's benevolent reassurance that self-discovery is an eternal process, *oh yippie*, I wished my *unfolding* would fix itself. I'd thought that by showing up at the concerts and facing my angst, I'd be free of my past. I thought I had arrived. In actuality, these concerts had only amplified my attachment to the band. Now I *really* wanted their attention. God Almighty, why was this so flippin' hard?

I was slowly maneuvering beyond my issues of unworthiness. Peeling away my ego-shadow felt like peeling an onion. It was happening in layers...and it made me cry. Yeah, I had slithered through some of my issues, but I still needed to get to the *core* of my fears.

Larry Byram, founder of Higher Alignment, describes the importance of healing our ego-shadow:

> When we heal our defensive identity, we learn to be with all types of people in a way that's open and nurturing of who they are without effort. We no longer have to define ourselves in terms of other people. We no longer operate protectively or reactively so that we can feel better about ourselves. Instead of having fear about others' reactions, we can relax into our being by seeing that their fears and desires come from their past. Instead of closing down when others judge us, imagine being able to open up and not take things personally. (*From Higher Alignment class handout*)

But how would I get there? Could music and rock concerts help me heal my fears? The recent concerts had brought my theories about unity, synchronicity, and the ego-shadow to a whole new level.

What *would* the world be like, I wondered, if there came a day when the human race was no longer defensive and ego-driven? What if we discovered we really are *hu*-man, and we acknowledged God in every other person, animal, and plant? Would we finally make nice with one another? Let's hope.

Back to the Boulder show for a moment. Rebecca, one of the intuitives participating in the psychic experiment, had stood in the balcony and taken copious notes. She emailed her observations a few days later...and added that the lead singer's sister had seen her notepad, come over and chatted a bit. The sister had then volunteered several things about his personal life, probably because she thought Rebecca was a reporter.

The guitarist, in fact, had mentioned halfway through the show that the singer's sister was in the audience, but he didn't indicate where she was. Upon hearing this, a woman next to the stage completely turned around and flashed *me* a radiant smile. I smiled back.

After the show, I meandered toward the entrance to touch base with Heidi and Rebecca and thanked them for participating in my experiment. En route to the coat check, I bumped into the woman who had smiled at me during the concert.

She had a coy grin on her face.

"Is your brother still here?" she asked.

Huh?

I'm an only child. I was totally caught off guard.

Completely bewildered, I stuttered, "Um…I…don't… have…a…brother."

Her face suddenly changed to rage, disbelief, or maybe embarrassment. She walked right past me without another word.

I got in line for my coat. *What the hell was that about?* A light bulb suddenly went off. *She thought I was the singer's sister!* Why would she think that? Geez, if we were related, he'd have to be my *little* brother since I'm three feet taller than him!

Wow. The Universe amazes me. What a perfect metaphor, a fan thinking *I* was family with a band member. Though not biologically related to TBIF, I *was* healing my funky fears and searching for possible past lives with them—an energetic *relationship*. Perhaps Jalynn the intuitive had been correct that the band and fans are a clan, a tightly knit group of souls? Maybe we really are one big happy eternal soul family travelin' along in a cosmic tour bus—just like the Partridge Family.

Before the Boulder concert, I had emailed the intuitives several questions. Heidi and Rebecca had sent their responses shortly after the concert. Here are a few highlights of my queries for them to observe, and their psychic impressions:

Did you pick up on any kind of unconscious message from TBIF to the fans?

Heidi: "By setting the energy of the music at red-to-orange colors (first and second chakras), they offer the audience plenty of permission to be themselves. The unconscious message is: 'Be bold. Be who you are.' Also, the band runs a lot of creative energy from their second chakras [creativity and sexuality center], which seems to open the audience's heart space. Again, the creative energy gives the permission to live outside the box…. The fans' response to the band's permission for the audience to have their dreams seems to create a sort of devotional loyalty."

Rebecca: "My impression is that the guitarist is the grounded shield behind which the other members can relax, feel protected, and express their creativity. The lead guitarist is the member who keeps the group grounded, and sets goals that the other members can work within."

During my radio-research days, statistics showed that people tend to listen to the music they've grown up with, particularly during their teen years. Is there a spiritual reason for this?

Rebecca: "Those are very powerful years of development, especially if it's a time when the person felt the most free and empowered. The music, in later years, then brings up feelings that tie to the earlier feelings of empowerment. Overall, my sense is that music and one's attraction to it have to do with inner vibration. If you are at a like vibration with a band, their energy, and their music, you become a fan. The fan may also grow in such a way that a band's music no longer resonates with the new self."

Wow! Being a fan was such a huge part of my identity that I couldn't imagine changing so much that my inner vibration would no longer resonate with TBIF.

Are there any pros or cons for fans to listen to the same music repeatedly over many years?

Heidi: "People seem to listen to the music that provides the vibration they want to incorporate into themselves. Likewise, bands often play the vibration they, too, want to own more fully. The vibration is the gift they are giving to themselves and others. People continue to listen to the music until they have absorbed that vibration.

"People who are born into a generation often have a similar lesson to learn. In that sense, there is a broad group agreement to explore a specific aspect of life. Hence, the music of a generation often holds the vibrational reminder of the purpose of the generation. In that way, people tend to listen to the music whenever they need to reconnect with meaning in their life."

There appears to be a significant reason why each of us is drawn to certain music. Rebecca and Heidi's comments support the idea that music reflects a congruent *inner vibration* that we either already own or want to incorporate into our being. Whether it's two psychic chicks at a rock concert, sound guru Jonathan Goldman, or Dr. Emoto's images of water exposed to rock songs, it's all about vibration.

What about past lives between the band and fans?

Rebecca: "Many of the band's fans have been led by the singer in a past life and still look to him for direction."

You've got to be kidding! Jalynn had said almost the exact the same thing years ago. He has a paternal, leader energy. I certainly hadn't picked up that vibe. Maybe that's why they're psychics and my middle name remains "Psychic Brick."

Then Heidi totally blew me away when she wrote that she sensed one of the band members was feeling "a level of pain and guilt" in my presence. PAIN AND GUILT IN MY PRESENCE? Oh, for the love of God! This was getting beyond absurd. Completely wig me out, why don't you? (Heidi knew nothing about my fear of rejection from the band, or how I had felt the very same guy had avoided eye contact with me over the past several years.)

Lastly, Anne noticed that a good portion of the crowd was almost rabid in their frenzied energetic connection with the guitarist, and he dished it out right back to them. She commented that the band and fans energetically were feeding off one another in a perpetual cycle. Heidi had also written that the fans and band seemed to have a devotional *loop* of energy.

This is an interesting observation because the word fan is an abbreviation for fanatic. Do some fans rely upon a band to provide them with that "music high" to such a degree that we become co-dependent? In this way, it can be a somewhat dysfunctional symbiotic relationship—fans and band—because we need each other to keep the emotional loop going. Noteworthy that both women had sensed this intense cyclical energy exchange.

So, should the fans begin a new twelve-step program *Rock 'n' Rollers Anonymous*? Sign me and my shadow right up!

CHAPTER 15

"THE SOUL AWAKENING"

—China Crisis

"A rock concert is in fact a rite involving the evocation and transmutation of energy."[36]

—William S. Burroughs, American novelist and
member of the Beat Generation

After my foray into the northwest concerts, Mommy Domestic Goddess returned home with the two kiddos. While cleaning toilets, all I could think about 24/7 was uncovering subconscious clues from TBIF's lyrics and unraveling this reincarnation mystery.

But my sanity was in question. Had I had crossed the line between obsession into possession? Was evil taking over my mind, causing irrational thoughts about past lives with a rock band, making me seem too far out even for *Jerry Springer*?

Yes, I'm a stark raving lunatic. Is that why I'm so *bleeping* happy?

Wake the Bleep Up got louder as synchronistic events continued slapping me upside the head while I meandered down the Rock 'n' Roll Yellow Brick Road. I whined to God, "Why don't other fans seem to have an inkling about their past lives with the band? I want someone to talk to."

Occasionally at concerts, the topic of writing a book came up, but I never divulged its contents. I didn't want to alienate myself by my big mouth blurting out that I was uncovering the hidden mysteries of the universe as a bona fide rock music reincarnation sleuth. I was dying to know if any other fans had similar woo-woo experiences as me, but I kept my large orifice shut and played the nice sane girl from Colorado.

After the Eugene, Oregon show, the fan nicknamed Sundante had also attended TBIF's next concert at the Roseland Theater in Portland, where we chatted again for awhile before the music started. She mentioned she'd like to keep in touch. Sure enough, a few weeks later she sent me an email asking how things were going.

Within a week of corresponding, Sundante and I had forged a trust. She wrote that she had something important to share, but was skittish to tell me for fear her "secret" would get out to other fans. I assured her that I was not with any "in" crowd and only socialized with other Superfans at concerts.

Eventually, I also felt comfortable enough to email her the essence of my rock 'n' roll metaphysical exploits. This was, in part, her response:

Laura…your email was so powerful that I must tell you I keep rereading it to gain strength from it. All the points you made were valid, and I KNOW they are true. It has really helped me tremendously.

Let's talk about intuition. It has been a powerful force in my life, too. I always had pictures in my head of my children. In fact, I chose my daughter's name when I was only seventeen. When I get a clear and unquestionable feeling, I KNOW it's true.

I think the most powerful instance was on a Friday night when I went to TBIF's bulletin board. I had been to some shows that week, but seldom read the boards. I was very new to it all. A certain person had a hyperlink to his own website, which I clicked on because I felt I had to. As it slowly downloaded, there was a photo of him standing among the boys in the band and, I swear to you, the moment I saw him, I quite literally said, "OH MY GOD" and pushed my chair away from the computer. The force was so powerful that I was completely shocked. It was like being struck by a bolt of lightning. The moment I saw HIM, I knew beyond a shadow of a doubt that he was the man I was meant to be with. That is crazy talk, but I know *you* can understand it. I KNEW. Absolutely NO DOUBT about it. So after reading a few things to learn about him, I sent him an email, because I HAD to. Thus began my relationship with [fan's name].

Yowza! Sundante's initial reaction at seeing a picture of another fan caught me by surprise. Yet I totally knew what had occurred. This instantaneous identification is often referred to in metaphysics as a **soul recognition**. According to past-life research, people often reincarnate with the same souls, such as friends and family members. Not only that, Danae had once said in a reading that our facial features reflect our past lives. Could it be that in our present life we actually look similar to a previous life? Therefore, might our souls subconsciously recognize one another?

According to Nora Amrani's website *Vibrani's One Source*, the recognition can be overwhelming:

Often meeting someone from your Oversoul can be a powerful experience, which may result in literal physical shaking. This triggers a soul or psychic shock, which shakes the cellular memory awake and shows a strong signal of how you resonate to the energy of meeting more of your Self. There is more than just a similarity between you. There is an unmistakable attraction, knowingness, and remembrance.[37]

This was amazing. I was writing about group reincarnation and Sundante appears to have had soul recognition with another devoted fan. My theory that the band drew people (souls) together in order to fulfill their karmic destinies or life purposes was being validated. The possible past-life associations were building. I thanked the Universe and the Law of Attraction for sending Sundante my way.

Here's another possible past-life soul recognition. A certain British musician is good friends with TBIF, and they have recorded several of his songs. In a book that chronicles the band's history, he wrote: "The first time I ever met [the band], I instantly felt like I had known them for years. Apart from their accents, they could have been fellow Brummies.... I would like to wish the band all the best of luck for their future, they deserve it. I like them a helluva lot, both as a band and as humans."[38]

I'd felt a strong, immediate resonance with Sundante when we first met, and now consider her part of my soul group. She felt the bond, too. For my fortieth birthday, she sent me a necklace with Sanskrit letters inscribed on a small rectangular piece of silver. On the back, the translation reads: *fearlessness.*

I also own a necklace with the Viking **Rune** symbol *Perth.* Runes are an ancient Nordic alphabet used as tools for divination. One of twenty-four symbols is etched into a stone, each representing a letter as well as eternal truths for self-understanding. I had been very drawn to the Perth symbol, which means: "Bringing something *hidden* to light."

That's my life in a nutshell. Raising the unconscious to the conscious. Bringing the unknown into the known.

When Sundante's necklace arrived, I immediately took off the Perth symbol and put on hers. I needed to be *fearless* to face the unknown ahead and to bring the message contained within this book to light.

It's not unusual for those who work with the Tarot to also be drawn to Runes. To us, all of this esoteric symbolic stuff is like Nirvana (Buddhist concept of heaven, not the grunge rock band).

Around this time, I constantly thought about symbols, alchemy, and the Tarot. I made up a short cheat sheet (okay, about twenty sheets) identifying each card, key word, geometrical association, numerology relationship, and how the essence of the cards might relate to my life, the band, and rock 'n' roll. My mind was constantly on the lookout for clues and associations between archetypes represented through the Tarot and music.

Epiphanies come at the darndest moments. Several times a week, shortly after falling asleep, I typically lurch wide-awake. Usually, I doze back off, but on this particular night, a connection between several TBIF album titles and the Tarot Major Arcana cards ripped through my mind.*

I was shocked to realize their second album title connects to the second card, the High Priestess; she is in color, but flanked on each side by a black-and-white column. Cool! It then dawned on me that the Tower card represents sudden upheaval, crisis, and being all shook up. Oddly enough, that concept mirrors TBIF's seventh album.

My memory shuffled through their album titles. Snap, crackle, POP! A flood light went off. Justice, the 11th card in the Universal Waite deck, represents balance and fairness; TBIF's eighth album title symbolizes balance and actually contains two *ones*, which numerically written become the number 11. The Death card symbolizes transition, rebirth, and moving on, a

---

*Note: the following descriptions may appear a bit cryptic since you may or may not know which band TBIF represents, and I'm not mentioning album/CD titles. It's not necessary to know any of that to read ahead, but feel free to decode the clues if you recognize which band it is. Part of the fun of going on a journey of self discovery is finding connections and figuring stuff out on your own.

shoe-in for TBIF's ninth album. The Fool is perfect for their tenth album; he is standing on the edge of the unknown. The Lovers are in the Garden of Eden, or the lap of luxury. The card is a dead ringer for TBIF's twelfth CD. The fifteenth card, the Devil, symbolizes the ego, a.k.a. a monster, and it incredibly matches TBIF's fifteenth album title!

My cells were lighting up like fireflies on a hot summer night. Ping…ping…ping…. This was too much fun! Now I *really* couldn't sleep!

The next day, I checked TBIF's website—22 albums were listed (in 2003). I subsequently associated *all* 22 Major Arcana cards with the 22 CD titles. Unbelievable!

Even unusual titles fit. TBIF's fourth album contains a word that sounds like *budo*; in Japanese it means "martial arts." Martial artists are disciplined protectors, and Japanese protectors and leaders are called Emperors. The Emperor is the fourth card in the Major Arcana! Budo also sounds like Buddha. In Sanskrit, *Budh* (Buddha) means enlightened or "awake." That fourth album made TBIF superstars…and *woke* the world up to their music. I guess **Wake the Bleep Up!** isn't my mantra by accident.

While we're on the subject of *waking the bleep up*, a photograph on the inside sleeve of the TBIF album I associated with the 11th card, Justice, depicts the singer and drummer standing and facing each other. Next to them, the guitarist and bassist are posed in the same manner. The way they are all standing makes them look like two ones, mirrored by another 1 1—or 11 11. This image of "ones" relates back to the album title.

Recently, many of my friends and I started seeing the numbers 11:11 everywhere: digital clocks, on odometers, or $11.11 on a receipt. According to numerous websites, 11:11 is an encoded *wake-up call* that supposedly triggers our memory to remind us of our mission in life. Many people who keep seeing 11:11 are referred to as **lightworkers**, "someone who feels compelled to help the earth in a spiritual way, through teaching, healing, prayer, writing and speaking, or some other way that sends light and love to others or the environment."[39] Was I a lightworker? Were TBIF lightworkers? Can numbers act as catalysts to help us Wake the Bleep Up!?

In numerology, 11 is referred to as a *master* number which possesses enormous potential, often coupled with a special pur- pose or mission in life. One of TBIF's band member's birth date reduces** to the number 11. This is called the Life Path number; the Life Path of an 11 means the person is highly intuitive. Such people have "the potential to be a source of inspiration and illu- mination for people. They are a channel for information.... Many inventors, artists, religious leaders, prophets, and leading figures in history have had the 11 prominent in their chart."[40]

Sundante, who does resonate with some of my metaphysi- cal theories, nevertheless found a few of my TBIF album associa- tions and numerology observations to be an "intuitive stretch." That's okay. I know I tend to be a bit out there—the intergalactic cosmos are my second home—but on *this*, I trusted that my intu- itive antennae were picking up important signals—indicating that I was on the right rock 'n' roll path of clues.

Everyone sees the world based on their own intentions and perceptions. For me, I had asked for a way to remember my soul identity and life path...and the Universe delivered BIG TIME, in the form of combining two of my passions—Tarot and TBIF. It was so much fun!

**Reducing a birthdate provides a digit to use for the Life Path number. For example, a person born on June 20, 1963 would determine their single number symbol by adding the following the numeric month, day and year: 6+ 2 +0+ 1 + 9 + 6 + 3 = 27. Now 2 + 7 = 9. (So, 9 is the Life Path num- ber). For a website to help calculate your own Life Path number and what it represents, check out www.decoz.com. Note: 11 and 22 are considered master numbers, and don't reduce to 2 and 4 respectively.*

So, did TBIF deliberately title their albums to reflect the Tarot cards? *That would probably be an intuitive stretch.* What's important is that these associations increased my trust in *my* own intuition.

The Universe provides us clues to the meaning of our life in the form of synchronicities. When I pay attention, the number of synchronicities increases. The interpretation of a synchronicity is unique for each person. Just as Sundante thought I'd gone a tad off the deep end with my revelations, for her, having a soul recognition with another fan was highly significant. Our souls lead us to the clues (synchronicities) that are meaningful for us—but they only offer meaning if we are open to perceiving them.

CHAPTER 16

"FEEL LIKE A NUMBER"

—Bob Seger

"Number is the Word but is not utterance; it is wave and light, though no one sees it; it is rhythm and music, though no one hears it. Its variations are limitless and yet it is immutable. Each form of life is a particular reverberation of Number."[41] —Maurice Druon, French novelist

Now that we've delved into numbers and numerology, let's get back to my fan survey. I'd asked fans for demographic data and feedback about their personal experiences with music. Lots of numeros. That part was easy. Inquiring if fans had a past life with their favorite band was not as simple. A question like that could get rotten tomatoes tossed at me. I ended up cleverly veiling the past-life queries, which saved me from feeling foolish and kept my sorry ass tomato free.

Past-life questions felt important to include in the survey. Many reincarnation case studies have asserted that an affinity, or an aversion, to a particular place or time period might be connected to a past life. Let's say you are a robust blonde, blue-eyed rock fan who never stepped foot in Africa—but anything African (music, art, food, the culture) gets your motor running. This *might* be suggestive of a past life. By this reasoning, if a large percentage of the fans were interested in a specific location or time period in history, it could suggest group reincarnation.

When I was twelve, movies on sixteenth and seventeenth-century Europe made me drool with lust. Men in puffy shirts, high black boots, and long curly wigs aroused my pre-teen fantasies. I remember feeling perplexed about why guys no longer strut around like Errol Flynn and Richard Chamberlain. When as an adult, a hypnosis session landed me in this time period, I finally understood my fascination with the Renaissance.

Most people don't go into a past-life regression with a particular era in mind. Usually, some significant crap is disturbing their psyche and they want to get it fixed. Sometimes hypnosis (or another therapy that accesses altered states of consciousness) is tried as a last resort to clear emotional turmoil. A time period and location are usually by-products of the subconscious journey, providing a context for understanding a compulsion or revulsion.

In my cyberspace survey, I quizzed two fan groups: TBIF fans, and fans of other classic rock bands from Aerosmith to Led Zeppelin. Forty-five TBIF fans and 115 fans of other bands responded. I used the general rock fans as a control group and looked for similarities and differences between the two fan bases. While sifting through my survey results, I tried to determine whether any consistent patterns had emerged among the fans that would indicate some past-life/present-life connection. It was a small, non-random sample, so possibly not statistically sound. Still, some interesting facts surfaced (see *www.soundofyoursoul.com* for survey questions and results).

What did I discover? Demographically, the fans were very similar. However, a higher percentage of TBIF female fans answered the survey (50%), as opposed to general rock fans (37%). The general-rock fans reflected the national radio format average; the typical classic-rock radio station's listener base is 35% female. TBIF most likely attracted more female fans because the good-looking dudes were icing on the cake—great musicians *and* eye candy.

A significant number of the TBIF respondents (over 70%) claimed they had met at least one band member, which was drastically higher than the general fans (28%), probably due in part to TBIF's intensive small-venue touring schedule over the past thirty years. TBIF fans had had a greater opportunity to bump into or meet band members and share group hugs.

As for popular geographic regions, England took top honors among both groups of fans. From other past-life research, many North Americans apparently recall lifetimes in Great Britain. I have been told by intuitives on several occasions that my own soul digs England, Scotland, and/or Ireland. This doesn't surprise me. When I lived in London twenty years ago, it felt like *home*. So many places evoked a sense of **déjà vu**.

Regarding time periods discovered with my fan survey, there was one unusual characteristic: Only 2% of general-rock fans said they were interested in the Civil War, compared to a whopping 27% of TBIF fans. The Civil War also turned up later as a possible lifetime for TBIF fans. However, due to the small number of responses, it could just be an anomaly. (Or maybe not!)

On to other findings. During my radio-research days, the following phrase was tossed around, as I referenced earlier in my queries to the three intuitive who attended the Boulder concert. "The music a person listens to between the ages of 15 to 20 is the music they will most likely listen to for the rest of their life." This phenomenon always bugged me because no other radio analysts could tell me *why* this happens.

The three intuitives had perceived that when a person resonates with a particular music, s/he remains a fan for a long time. However, if that person's inner vibration changes, s/he may no longer connect with that music.

To further address this question, my survey asked the age that the person became a fan of their favorite band. Guess what?

Even in my miniscule sample, the median age that a general rock fan got tweaked was 15.8; for TBIF fans, 15.9—just as the radio truism had predicted. I myself was 15 when TBIF's music unlocked the nucleotides in my own DNA.

Why do some of us get swept away by a band at an early age? When I asked myself, the word "imprinting" popped into my noggin. Imprinting? Using ducks as an example, one of my college psychology class lectures explained imprinting in this way: Shortly after hatching, there is a window of time when baby ducklings regard a moving animal nearest to them as Mom. But what if Momma duck isn't around, and a meandering pig is in the vicinity? Baby duckling sees the sow and thinks, "Mom, where have you been all of my life?" and runs quacking and nipping at alternate Mom's hooves, thoroughly bewildering Ms. Piggy.

Imprinting is instinctual. By providing a safe guardian to closely follow, it helps to ensure a young animal's survival. Humans also appear to have a language "imprinting window" during infancy and early childhood. That's why we pick up speech patterns and second languages more easily as children.

Here's my off-the-wall theory: what if people have an imprinting window during their teen years, when some of us seem to unconsciously transfer the imprinted archetype of our parents onto our favorite rock band? Based upon my survey and the radio aphorism, if a 15- to 16-year-old human hears and res-onates with Van Halen's music (for example), it's not such a leap that they would imprint musicians as "parent." Then for the rest of their lives, they run after David Lee Roth and Eddie Van Halen, subconsciously yelling, "Momma! Momma!"

Is this why so many of us at forty and fifty are still follow-ing the same rock band? Were we imprinted by the band and their music?

Yeah, I think so. This Superfan was *waaay* imprinted.

If imprinting stamps the impression of "parent" onto a young animal for the purpose of protection, as some teenagers transition into adulthood and leave the security of their parents' guidance, is it possible they'd latch onto a band as a surrogate protector? The Universe had drawn me to TBIF's music when I was fifteen—several months *before* my mom launched the torpedo that my father was dying of pancreatic cancer. Nature abhors a vacuum; so when the archetype of the father is missing in our lives, I believe we may subconsciously imprint a surrogate parent to fill the void. Looks like my psyche latched onto the men in TBIF. They were the prominent male figures in my world when my biological father departed from my life. Plus, they played music I loved, which kept me hooked!

But a parent's death or absence isn't the only trigger for *imprinting*, which seems to have occurred to millions of people. Just look at what happened to KISS fans. When I asked survey fans to list their top three favorite other bands as teenagers (after their numero uno band), KISS won hands down as the next most popular band among TBIF fans. Yet KISS wasn't mentioned *once* as a second or third favorite after any other group or artist.

Since so many TBIF fans enjoyed KISS as teens, I decided to see KISS in concert myself. Yikes! Let's just say that I was not imprinted in any way, shape, or form by their music or costumes. To me, KISS is not momma duck!

Nevertheless, KISS remains one of the top grossing concert bands of all time, due to their incredibly large, loyal fan base; fanatics refer to themselves as members of the KISS "army." Out of the thousands of KISS soldiers in attendance the night I went to a concert, Gawk Girl was the only soul who didn't know the lyrics to every song. Warning: Do not chow down a nutritious Cliff bar, pound back a cold can of mango-juice nectar, and read *The Hidden Messages in Water* while relaxing in a lawn seat while the warm-up band, Poison, performs on stage—if you want to blend in with other KISS soldiers. I stuck out like an ulcerated thumb.

Yet, as you may recall, several intuitives have seen me as a "soldier" in other lifetimes with TBIF. On that strange planet with the orange sky, Jalynn had sensed we were planning for a battle. Danae had seen us as brothers fighting off-planet to liberate a group of people. In my first reading with Danae, she had channeled: "This soul group that you are a part of moves with the vibrational wave of their music. It is one of thousands of soul groups incarnated at this time. So understand the calling that you feel is akin to the calling of all soul groups moving as armies of light, legions of light."

The calling we feel—that intense, passionate yearning to be together at concerts and scream at the top of our lungs the words to every song—ensured that we joined together again in this lifetime. The music and possible imprinting compel us to come together. Perhaps there is some kind of soul connection between KISS and TBIF "armies"?

As to the question of why KISS fans are so loyal, imprinting is the most logical explanation. It provides a one-two punch: the first hit is visual, the second aural. KISS costumes and black-white face paint create archetypal superheroes. Since it seems that we are susceptible to imprinting during our teen years, this guise has kept many fans devoted to KISS long into adulthood.

Regarding the imprint of sound, I've never considered the guys in KISS to be extraordinary musicians or songwriters, though KISS fans would beg to differ. What's important is that the combination of their appearance and hard-rock sound lured male teenagers, much like the Sirens (those sexy babe-a-licious singing Greek sea nymphs) had lured Odysseus. If you are imprinted with a band's music, you're hypnotically drawn to their sound, seemingly forever.

So from our soul's perspective, what is the point of all this? If we are armies of light, how does TBIF or any other rock band's music help us heal? Favorite word of the day: VIBRATION. I believe that all music displays the healing power of *sound*, but *only* to those people who match the resonance or frequency.

KISS's music was totally not appealing (or healing) to me. But obviously for thousands of other souls, it is. Why? Because what helps *me* heal is not necessarily what helps *you* heal.

Our society is like *Goldilocks and the Three Bears* when it comes to music. Some of us like it soft, some like it hard, others find the middle of the road just right. I believe that's because our souls have jumped into this lifetime with all different kinds of crap to heal, and different vibrations help us to shift our consciousness. Imprinting is one way for many of us to become connected to the healing force of music, no matter our level of awareness or the experience of our soul.

So if imprinting is instinctual and helps to assure the survival of the individual (be it a person or a duck), then how would being imprinted by our favorite band during our teen years assist our ability to survive? Perhaps it's not about physical survival, but more about exceeding our potential and rising towards self-actualization.

Maybe imprinting a band is beneficial in that it allows us to tap into feelings of joy. More than any other response to the survey, fans commented that seeing their band in concert produced intense emotions such as bliss and elation. Some mentioned the word *ecstatic*. One Rolling Stones fan wrote that seeing them in concert was *OrgasMICK*. Self-actualized people tend to feel jubilant, because they sense a deep connection to themselves and others.

According to many spiritual teachings, bliss, joy, and

empowerment signify being in the highest enlightened state. Even studies based upon the connection between attitude and physical well-being show that a happy person is more likely to live longer. Makes sense. If we are joyful, odds are we will flow with life and contribute to society. If we are habitually frustrated and angry, we're more prone to acts of rage and violence, stress and illness, which doesn't do a lot to increase our odds of survival.

Nevertheless, I still question why we possibly imprint a band at about age fifteen or sixteen? Is it because our emotional baggage originated during childhood? By our mid-to-late teenage years, the primary psychological complexes we developed as kids are entrenched. Then we have the remainder of our lives to learn and grow from these issues, so we can move toward joy.

Months after writing this, I leafed through an issue of *Time* magazine about the adolescent brain: "During adolescence you get fewer but faster connections in the brain.... The brain becomes a more efficient machine, but there is a trade-off: it is probably losing some if its raw potential for learning and its ability to recover from trauma."[42] By our teen years, we don't process trauma as readily. Doesn't it make sense that to help us cope and heal, music is the perfect antidote?

One last thing. Why are some fans drawn to see a band perform live over and over again? My survey shows that some Grateful Dead fans had seen upwards of 500 concerts. The average TBIF fan had attended 23 shows.

Why is live so much better than Memorex? One possibility is resonance, which literally means "to sound again, to echo." We resonate with one another, because people vibrate and emit energetic signals all the time. Just ask the Beach Boys. They've got "Good Vibrations." Elvis was "All Shook Up." In the 1950s, people started to "Shake, Rattle, and Roll." Since everything vibrates, the Law of Attraction is based upon *resonance*...and another similar concept, **entrainment**.

Entrainment is like a Vulcan mind-meld. When two similar objects are in close proximity, the object of weaker vibration will match, (or entrain) to the object of stronger vibration. For example, clock pendulums of different lengths begin to synchronize with the strongest pendulum.

According to Jonathan Goldman, "Entrainment is an aspect of sound that is closely related to rhythms and the way these rhythms affect us.... Entrainment also takes place when two people have a good conversation. Their brain waves oscillate synchronously. Such entrainment is seen in the relationship between students and their professors. Psychotherapists and clients entrain with each other, as do preachers and their congregation."[43]

If teachers and students, preachers and their congregations, therapists and clients are entrained, is it such a leap to conclude that rock musicians and their fans are riding the entrainment train, too? All aboard the "Marrakesh Express!"

When entrainment takes place, there is always an exchange of energy and information. Now, think of a typical nuclear family. Children are physically the smaller, weaker "object" and usually entrain with the stronger, dominant vibration of their parents. As we mature and our own vibration strengthens, some of us as teens were drawn to rock concerts. Was it because the musicians were sending us messages (information) and the louder, or stronger, vibration (band) entrained our still weaker vibration (fan) into synchronization? That may be one reason why rock concerts are so frickin' loud! The vibrations needed to be super strong to entrain thousands of fans, so that we began to **Wake the Bleep Up!**

When I first read about entrainment, it brought to mind drumming, which has long been a tool for resonance in traditional cultures. The rhythms induce trance states for the tribal shaman or healer, and also revved up the warriors as they went off to battle. In his book *Drumming at the Edge of Magic*, Grateful Dead drummer Mickey Hart writes, "Percussion was almost universally used during such rituals of transition as birth, puberty, marriage, and death, when the spirit world is called upon for guidance."[44]

The drum *entrains* our physical rhythms—heartbeat, respiration, etc. But isn't it interesting that percussion instruments are also used during important periods of transition, such as puberty? In modern western society, at the end of puberty, the most significant rite of passage into adulthood is getting our driver's license. Big whoop.

Could we become imprinted with a rock band during our teen years due to a lack of initiation rituals, which, for thousands of years, were accompanied by a drummer's funky tribal beat? These rituals are missing from our modern society. Did we replace them with rock concerts?

Let's recap my observations:

- Ducks imprint because they instinctually need parental guidance.
- Teenagers may imprint bands because we, too, still need guidance.
- Music is an encoded vibration; sound is a carrier wave of information.
- Drums emit a powerful pulse that creates entrainment and, with entrainment, there is always an exchange of energy and information.
- In native cultures, drumming calls on the spiritual world for guidance during important rituals.
- Do drum-focused rock bands help exchange spiritual energy and information with fans?

If the intuitives' psychic compasses were on target, and a subconscious signal is being emitted from a band's instruments and the singer's voice, then physical presence might be an important factor to feel the resonance, or entrainment, with the musicians. Recorded music doesn't go far enough. If some fans are drawn to a singer because he played follow-the-leader with them in another lifetime, then being physically present and soaking up his energy could be key for their healing.

So the next time you want a new pick-up line, ask, "Hey, baby, wanna be part of my army and get entrained with me?" It works for rock stars.

CHAPTER 17
"TOO MUCH INFORMATION"
—Duran Duran

*"When I'm singing and in touch with the energy I'm gener-
ating, I sometimes literally have no awareness of where I am.
The Ego disappears, and me and my surroundings with it....
that's the reason I'm in music—to achieve that feeling."*[45]
—Daryl Hall, musician

Have some rock fans had past lives with members of a band?
Your ego may say, "Reincarnation is cow poop." My ego agrees
with yours. Perhaps they should date? It's hard to fathom how a
part of us could survive death and come back again in another
body.

That's because the soul, not the ego, is eternal. Our ego dies
with us when our body expires. No wonder the ego freaks out
about death. However, the following experience helped to chip
away my own ego's tremendous skepticism regarding reincarnation and the possibility of soul groups.

KISS may have black and white face paint, but the alchemical
connection to TBIF's black-and-white checkerboard motif began
driving me loco. How could this simple logo be such a powerful
image for me? Did I really have any past-life association with it?

I made an appointment with the folks at Psychic Horizons,
a local intuitive training center. I psyched myself up for the session by talking to the Big Guy upstairs. *Please show me if my soul
has a past-life connection to alchemy. This dark and light theme
seems like a huge clue, and I need to know. Am I going down the*

wrong Yellow Brick Road? Is my psychic compass screwed up, or what?

At the center, I found myself in a room with three student psychics who did my reading in turns. They went through my chakras and related what they saw. I felt that, though we'd never met, each woman tapped into my energy very accurately.

Intuitive #1: "There is a desire, yearning. Oh, the quest, the Holy Grail. What would that bring you? Contentment. You are going through a really big growth period. The next step is opening up your own clairvoyance and having certainty in your own perceptions and intuitions, giving that space and honor."

Intuitive #2: "People are attracted to you. You have a kind of magnetism. It is for healing. This is a leadership quality, ideology—a vision. People want that for themselves. You give them permission to be who they are and to evolve."

Yes, I am searching for the Rock 'n' Roll Holy Grail, and some friends do refer to me as "Dear Abby." But at the end of the session, I asked the group my one and only question. "Imagine a black-and-white checkerboard pattern. Is there any past-life connection between me and (names of members of TBIF) and the checkerboard image?" I waited with bated breath, screaming the word *alchemy* in my mind.

Intuitive #2: "There is a connection. I see the four of them, plus you, in a séance doing some kind of Voodoo. This black-and-white checkerboard thing is doing something with dark and light. Might be something light, like using a Ouija board to try to cross the veils. Something about getting involved in the dark arts. Somehow, all of you want to create clarity around the whole situation. Maybe somehow to make amends for something that went awry, something you feel guilty about."

Intuitive #3: "It looks like the group of you are doing something occultish. Alchemy is the word I keep hearing."

"Oh, My God!!" I gasped.

"It looks like some kind of fraternal, brotherly connection between all of you guys," she continued. "You made some agreements in that lifetime to work on."

I became totally unglued and started sobbing. The women gave me a moment to collect myself.

Intuitive #1: "I see a life where they are all males and you were a female. There are a lot of odd-man-out pictures, exclusionary pictures, pictures about what that meant in that social realm. So, you are in a female body and not in the club. They were in male bodies, so they *are* the club. Lots of pictures of them leaving you. Older brother, little sister, constantly leaving you. One lifetime is set in a small-town prairie. There are two levels. One, you have this fear that they are going to leave you by necessity, maybe they go to war. The other is by choice; they leave you because they want to."

Intuitive #3: "It looks like part of the agreement was that you all worked together so closely, and it was very important that what you were doing not be blabbed around or known by the public, to keep it secret in your group. Because you made that agreement so strongly and energetically to each other, it bled through as spirits. You made an agreement that said: 'We are in this for eternity, because this is a big deal.'"

The psychics then asked, "Did this reading have any relevance to your current life?" After Aqualung girl stopped snotting, I cried, "Yes!"

But what they saw, was it really true? Some past-life researchers suggest that events are literal, while others regard them as figurative interpretations of the psyche. However, the accuracy of the energy these three intuitives picked up on was beyond freaky for me.

When listening to a tape of the session several months later,

I realized I'd been so focused on their information about the checkerboard that I'd missed the part when Intuitive #2 had said people were drawn to me because of my ability to help them heal. This now felt significant. I had already been a student of numerous healing modalities over the years, yet never practiced professionally out of fear of not being good enough.

When she related that I had to make amends for something that went awry, something I felt guilty about, a red flag went up. As a child, I had an obsessive fear of making mistakes. Everything was my fault. Even Nixon's impeachment, and I was only eleven. Contrary to what you may be thinking, my parents were always supportive of me, and they rarely yelled or made me feel wrong. My dementia was all my own.

But now I did wonder. Had my subconscious retained memories of a past life when I screwed around with other people's lives? Had I engaged in dark arts in another life? What goes around, comes around. That's karma. If it were true, did I learn right from wrong?

The theme of the guys abandoning me was far too significant to pass off as just another figment of my imagination. *Little sister!* TBIF sang a song years ago about a little sister...and the woman at the Boulder concert thought I was the singer's sister! This is too bizarre. However, rejection was also a theme as a concubine in the Middle East, and Old England as revolutionary writers. Now those possible lifetimes of abandonment and betrayal reared their ugly head again and made me kind of queasy.

I had thought the Boulder concert moved me past my fear of rejection, but this triple reading triggered some major karmic doo-doo. Funky, twisty knot in stomach.

Just when you think it's safe to go back in the water, that you have mastered a life lesson, your soul says, "Think you're done with that issue? Ha! It's time to work through another layer—if you dare." Of course, the dares get bigger with each level. So do the stomach pains.

In this lifetime, TBIF's music felt vital to my existence. Would I learn to stop clinging to their energy or worrying that I was making a huge mistake by writing about reincarnation? (Bad girl. We took an oath. Shhhhhh! It's a secret!) Sorry, the reincarnation cat's leaping out of the bag, so you better stock up on some Meow Mix.

If what those three intuitives had sensed was real, I would be breaking the oath big time with this book. Oh no, here comes another wave of those funky stomach knots again.

And what about Intuitive #2's impression of me doin' Voodoo? Mega trippy. Driving home, I almost had to stop the car and pull over. An epiphany was whacking me on my frontal lobe. "The Doctor! That's one of the clues!"

The Doctor you say? What Doctor? Dr. Doolittle? Dr. Kildare? Dr. Seuss? Dr. Dre? No, no, no, I say, I say. A TBIF album from the mid-1980s had a colorful caricature on the cover of a *witch doctor*. The guitarist, with his sarcastic wit, had said in an interview, "…That's me on the front, that's how I look in the morning."[46]

Another distant image floated down my memory lane. In the 1980s, the band had made a music video in which a woman stabbed needles into a doll that resembled the singer, while he grabbed his leg with the pang of each needle. A *Voodoo* doll.

So Psycho Girl went directly to the computer to look up Voodoo and witch doctors on the Internet. Would I find a link between Voodoo and the black-and-white checkerboard?

Not exactly. I discovered that Voodoo is still widely practiced in Haiti, and in 1800, Haiti was the richest colony in the world. Snotty white folks had imported Africans and forced them into slavery. After a twelve-year struggle, the black Haitian slaves eventually kicked out the butts of the invading Spanish, British, and French armies. A revolution of 500,000 blacks against 50,000 whites for freedom. The black-and-white checkerboard came to mind. A metaphor, not literal? Black and white people, not squares?

For months, I scoured the Internet trying to uncover any symbol remotely related to the checkerboard, but nothing matched. However, I did uncover a lot more about Voodoo than I cared to know. The thought of a possible soul connection to Voodoo's darker side made my stomach twist further into funkier knots. *If I need to heal a subconscious memory, let's face this puppy.* So I pushed onward.

In *The Secret Power of Music*, author David Tame states that "Jazz and the blues were the parents of rock and roll, this also means that there exists a direct line of descent from the Voodoo ceremonies of Africa, through jazz, to rock and roll and all other forms of rock music current today."[47]

And, yes, the intuitive had seen me doing Voodoo without knowing that I was writing a book about rock 'n' roll. My stomach pains skyrocketed.

Tame believes that rock music is evil. But how can something that brings so much joy be sinister? It is discomforting to consider rock music a detriment to our society—but the Voodoo fixation gnawed at me. I'm not evil incarnate now, but had I been involved in the dark arts in a past life? Had something gone awry...and was I feeling guilty about it now?

UGGGHH! Pass the Rolaids!

Had I been involved in the Haitian revolution? I wondered. And did this have anything to do with New Orleans, where Voodoo is still practiced? TBIF has a song about Mardi Gras. Connections, connections.

Then I had a dream. A snail with two heads told me it was called a *comet*. Comet? Co—meaning two?

When I woke up, I looked up comet in an online etymology dictionary. It's French, meaning "long-haired star." That cracks me up. Mucho rock stars have long hair! Curiously, the words in TBIF's name stem from the French...and Haiti was a *French* colony.

Around this time, I came upon an intriguing book titled *Past Lives of Famous People* by David Bengston. By accessing the **Akashic records**, Bengston believes that musician John Lennon has had several influential lifetimes, ranging from Russian revolutionary communist leader Vladimir Lenin, to Abraham Lincoln's assassin, John Wilkes Booth. I had emailed Mr. Bengston about my rock-music group-reincarnation insights, and asked if he might check into TBIF's past lives for my book. He saw a connection for the four of them to a former group of French musical entertainers hundreds of years ago.

Charol, the clairvoyant, had seen TBIF as traveling minstrels or troubadours; and medieval France was a breeding ground for wandering musicians. Mr. Bengston told me that many rock stars have had previous lives involving music, though most weren't famous or in history books.

David Tame wrote, "Minstrels were the Middle Ages' equivalent of the rock or folk-rock musician: they dressed and lived as hippies, their numbers grew constantly and they met together in gigantic gatherings or 'fests.' The minstrels very powerfully affected the social climate of their day."[48]

I strongly suspect that history might be repeating itself. According to my survey, the general-rock fans cited the Middle Ages and the Renaissance as the time periods to which they were most drawn outside of the twentieth century. Next to Great Britain, rock fans cited France as one of the top places to which they were attracted. And don't forget men's coiffed long hair of the Middle Ages—the staple for modern rock stars, and *comets*. Now if only these guys would wear puffy shirts and high black boots. I'm such a Renaissance Girl.

Medieval Girl has way too much information in her head: a possible Voodoo past life filled with the dark arts, fraternal secrets and oaths; abandonment and rejection from TBIF in other life-times; unidentified guilt since childhood; and some bizarre French connections to rock music and the Renaissance. Forget the Rolaids. I need a vacation.

CHAPTER 18

"SYNCHRONICITY"

—The Police

"The musician is very close to mysticism, far closer than the philosopher. In fact, music comes closest, as far as expressing the truth is concerned, because music is meaningful without any words; it is meaningful simply because it rings some bells in your heart. The great music is that which creates a synchronicity between you and itself, when your heart starts resonating in the same way, when you start pulsating in the same way."[49] —Osho, Indian mystic and philosopher

Sometimes synchronistic messages, like intuitive insights, don't initially make sense. Patience and trust are essential ingredients for allowing such messages to unfold. It's called **Divine Timing**, and stems from higher consciousness. Our soul communicates with a **field of intelligence**, then brings us intuitive hits and tingles at the right moment.

I'm learning there is often a deeper meaning or symbolism to eventually be discovered. There's a richness that comes from letting clues unfold—an understanding that deepens because we didn't hastily jump to conclusions. We're not supposed to figure it all out at once, so our soul teases us with bits and pieces to keep us interested and to peak our curiosity.

Where will the clues lead? Your guess is as good as mine, but I trust that my soul knows what the hell it's doing.

Synchronicity often weaves its way into our experience when we least expect it. Like when we're on vacation. My hubby, our two young daughters, and I drove to my in-laws' house in northern Idaho for our annual summer visit. I lugged my new TBIF CD, the Tarot and Oracle cards, several books, and a bunch of highlighters to mark all of the important pearls of wisdom these tomes would offer. I even took my dream journal, sensing I might need it. I had unconsciously prepared for events to come that would make me stand back and take yet another different look at reality.

It all began with vacation book #1: actor Richard Chamberlain's memoir *Shattered Love*. Since I was twelve, Mr. Chamberlain has been the primary go-to guy for my fantasies, in part because he wore those puffy shirts in *The Three Musketeers*, *The Man in the Iron Mask*, and *The Count of Monte Cristo* (and they all take place in France!). And, yes, I'm aware that Mr. Chamberlain is gay, but in my daydreams he digs tall women who write strange books about reincarnation and rock 'n' roll.

Anyhow, his memoir blew me away because he is an incredibly spiritual guy, and he wrote about some of the exact same metaphysical concepts I'm covering here. Cool! Maybe I was drawn to RC because I intuitively sensed his spiritual awareness. His writings gave me not only a peek into his soul, but whisked me off on a trail of totally trippy synchronistic events.

Uncannily, Richard Chamberlain wrote about the numerous checkerboard patterns he had noticed when traveling through Bali. My checkered flag went up!

The next day after reading that, I met a woman who was selling jewelry at a flea market, who told me that her pretty earrings had been made in Bali. Wow. (A definite synchronicity.) I skedaddled back to my in-laws' house to their computer in the loft, hoping to find my own Bali/checkerboard connections.

The checkerboard that RC referred to matched the description of a poleng cloth, a black-and-white checkered material wrapped around statues of gods and demons in many temples and shrines. The black-and-white design signifies the tug between good and evil, the sacred and the profane. This motif not only shows up in the writings of European alchemists during the Renaissance and at NASCAR races, but also halfway around the world in Indonesia! So, this *was* an important universal *archetype*.

Archetypes popped up in several of the books I had brought along, including Michael S. Schneider's *A Beginner's Guide to Constructing the Universe*. My highlighter tripped over another fascinating nugget. He wrote that the chessboard was,

> consciously designed to represent our world of transformations.... Each step on the board, represented by the movement of the pieces, takes us through the polarities of the **Dyad**, light and shadow, the eternal struggle between consciousness and unconsciousness, wisdom and ignorance, our constructive and destructive motivations. We walk among opposite forces waging battle for domination of the world and Self, engaging in the struggle for spiritual enlightenment that is the unseen significance of each of our lives.[50]

A super-duper AHA!

So, I'm attracted to a rock band that uses the black-and-white chessboard image on their albums, guitars, and merchandise—and it just so happens that the origins of the chessboard are spiritually based? And I've been led to write a book about spirituality and rock music? How freaky is that????

But I wanted to know more about the checkerboard. In what country or geographic location was this image significant for *me* in other lifetimes? Since clueless is my middle name, I consulted the Tarot and JC.

Now that I'd been working with the cards for over a year, I'd come to trust the information I intuited from them. The randomly selected cards always told a story or offered answers to my questions. Since the images are archetypal, any element might spark an insight.

This time, two of the cards I pulled (8 of Cups, 3 of Wands) contained lots of mountains and rivers. I had noted the 3 of Wands previously in the spread about the strange TBIF "Colorado" song with the lyrics about a river, south, east, riddles, and clues. The suit of Cups represents west; wands are south. More possible geographical hints?

Since *where* was difficult to pin down, I asked *when*. Each card would represent a digit: I pulled four cards, assuming I had a significant lifetime in the past 1000 years. I got *1841*.

A chill sprinted down my spine. I remembered 1841 cropping up in a dream. Wow. I rummaged through my dream journal, and found the reference from nine months earlier. This was getting creepy.

A train went through a big group of hotels. Some people kept talking about a convention in Missouri. Now the train transformed into a subway. A book was on a table and it looked like a scrapbook, but old, and it was about Abe Lincoln's life. He was born in Missouri or something about 1841 when he was born or died. The book was "alive," like a three-dimensional hologram. I had to take a test on the book in reverse, starting at the end.

Over the past six years, I had recorded a half-dozen dreams in which I was in the Old West during the 1800s. In many cases, a dream turned into a sepia image snapshot, as if it were an antique photo from a century ago. At other times, images started as a static picture, then turned into a holograph, then transformed into a movie.

The distorted sequencing of time and motion had always gotten my attention. Perhaps I had taken the test in reverse because I had to go backwards in time?

Hooked on finding answers, I traveled back in time via the Internet. Sites reported that Abe Lincoln hadn't been born in Missouri, nor had anything stupendous occurred in 1841. The only thing fairly significant in U.S. history that year was the beginning of "Manifest Destiny." *Go west young woman.* And in this lifetime I had—to my favorite state, Colorado.

The clues thus far: black and white, checkerboard, alchemy, Voodoo, France, Haiti, slaves, war, Abe Lincoln, Missouri, 1841, subway, east, west, south. Any patterns? Nope. But, neigh, hold your horses. Maybe there are a few connections.

The overall theme of the group-reincarnation books I had read focused on soul group trauma. Many past-life memories involved being persecuted, for religious beliefs or ethnic differences.

Black slaves in Haiti had been persecuted; the slaves in the good ol' US of A weren't much better off. And who had emancipated the slaves? President *Abraham Lincoln.* A Civil *War* had broken out between the North and the *South* in the *east*ern part of the United States. And how had the slaves escaped to the north? By UNDERGROUND RAILWAY (*subway*)!

Not only that, several research sites noted how suicide was common, both with black Haitians and African slaves en route to the new world. While "suicide" was not on my current clue list, it got my attention because this theme permeates certain early TBIF songs. It was also something I had seriously considered during my seventh-grade year in hell.

Had I been driven to commit suicide in some previous lifetime? I wondered. I turned to my new deck of **Tao Oracle cards** (a divination system similar to Tarot, but based upon the Chinese I Ching) to show me a picture of what race or nationality I was if I had committed suicide in a past life. Shuffle, shuffle, split deck, turn card over.

Completion. Verrrry interesting. A *black* runner is crossing a finish line at the end of a marathon. This was an *Asian* Oracle deck, in which only a few cards featured black-skinned people.

Something also kept bugging me about Missouri. The Internet revealed that a small black slave population had lived in Missouri…and many had fought in the Civil War. Had any infantry insignias included a black-and-white checkerboard? Nope, nada. Time to rest my weary eyes.

But what's that sound? Actor Matthew Broderick?

I peeked over my in-laws' loft railing. Mr. Broderick was on the downstairs television, dressed in a soldier's uniform, and talking to a group of black men. I asked my mother-in-law what she was watching.

"*Glory.* It's a really good movie about blacks fighting in the Civil War."

NO BLEEPING WAY! A huge cosmic ha-ha. It's also kinda weird that a high percentage of TBIF fans who answered my survey were interested in the Civil War.

What was this? Synchronicity #909?

909 reminded me of the song "One after 909" by the Beatles. TBIF's music was highly influenced by the Fab Four…and John Lennon. In fact, two of the guys in TBIF had worked briefly with Mr. Lennon shortly before he was assassinated. What if, if, if, if, as reported in David Bengston's past-life book, his insight held merit? What if John Lennon had been John Wilkes Booth, who shot *Abe Lincoln*?

I'd gotten clues about possible lifetimes as a Haitian or American slave, and a black Civil war soldier. What was next, an oppressed American Indian? Um…you betcha.

CHAPTER 19

"LAST NIGHT I HAD THE STRANGEST DREAM"

—Simon and Garfunkel

"Truly fertile Music, the only kind that will move us, that we shall truly appreciate, will be a Music conducive to Dream, which banishes all reason and analysis. One must not wish first to understand and then to feel. Art does not tolerate Reason."[51]

—Albert Camus, Nobel prize winner, French-Algerian author,
philosopher, and journalist

For several months, my dreams went AWOL. No more total recall. Most nights, I was in a vast, dark void. But in Idaho, an incredibly vivid reverie catapulted me out of my nice warm bed at the unholy hour of five in the morning:

I went to see TBIF in concert, wearing sneakers and no black sparkly hat. I looked in a restroom mirror. Blue eyeliner was smeared under my eye, on my teeth and lips. It wouldn't rub off. Damn.

Then, I was in the audience staring at the singer's right eye. I zoomed in on his pupils. His eye was really large. He sang the words "Meggie's Dead" over and over, very slowly, like a funeral dirge.

Suddenly, TBIF started playing the song "Helter Skelter" really fast and they ran all over the stage, throwing and sliding things like wrenches and pipes to one another.

Each guy knew what tool he needed, as if they were perform-
ing a ritual.

Part of a word was spelled with bullet holes on a wall
behind the stage. The guitarist handed me a gun to finish the
word, but I passed the gun to another fan. The letters of the
word were only partially formed: T R U E or T R U C E.

What in the world was my subconscious trying to communicate to me?

The blue eyeliner was on my mouth. Blue represents the
color of our throat chakra, which is associated with communica-
tion, self-expression, emotions, and *rituals*. Did I have communi-
cation issues with the band? Ya got that right.

And who the *bleep* was Meggie? Me in another life? Does she
have anything to do with 1841, Haiti, or the Civil War? How
could I figure out where Meggie had lived?

A fantabulous idea was sparked by the world globes in my
mother-in-law's loft. Let's play *National Geographic!* I closed my
eyes, set an intention to find the location, spun the mini-earth,
and put down my finger. I opened my eyes. My index finger was
on the southern part of *South* Dakota, *almost* touching Colorado
or *Missouri.* TBIF's "Colorado" song included the word south.
Was South a clue? My psychic compass was spinning in all directions.

Back to the dream. Zooming in on the singer's eye could
signify a shift in focus—from the slow funeral-like music to the
sped-up version of "Helter Skelter." Research Girl looked up
Helter Skelter on Wikipedia and saw a disturbing entry. Murderer
Charles Manson had claimed that the song "Helter Skelter" was a
secret coded message from the Beatles to start a *war* in which
black Americans would rise up and wipe out all snotty *white*
folks. Secret codes in rock music? Geez, who in their right mind
would think *that* could possibly be true? Divine Timing would

soon reveal the answer.

What about rituals, pipes, and wrenches in the dream? Years ago, I dreamed of pipes. Thank heavens I brought my dream journal to Idaho. Look what I found.

> *The guitarist got my attention. I was supposed to sword fight him, but I didn't have a sword, so I was trying to do it with metal pipes and stuff. This seemed to be some part of a ritual.*

The band and the word *ritual* had appeared in both pipe dreams. Did the ritual have to do with the words TRUE or TRUCE?

Peace pipe popped into my head. On the Internet, I found that the peace pipe was used in Native American *rituals* to bring a *truce* between fighting tribes. The four directions—east, south, west, north—were also an essential part of the ceremony.

I asked the Oracle cards what may have happened in South Dakota. Any connection to 1841, or the TBIF "Colorado" song about riddles, rivers, and looking out to the south and east? Shuffle, shuffle, shuffle.

I turned over the *Deliverance* card. You won't believe it, Tonto. An American Indian is standing under a lightening-filled sky. The card means *liberation* and *freedom*. In 1841, South Dakota was teeming with Native Americans, the Oglalas, looking for liberation and freedom from us snotty white folks. But look what I found in *The Oglala People, 1841-1879: A Political History.*

> The Oglalas faced a major political upheaval in 1841 when Bull Bear, a prominent *itancan* and holy man, was murdered during an intratribal quarrel. In the wake of his death, the Oglalas divided into two major sociopolitical factions—the Bear people and the Smoke people.[52]

Whoa. So 1841 *was* a significant year—for Dakota Indians. Sounds as though they were in dire need of a peace pipe, too.

The intuitive Danae had seen the past life with me and a band member fighting off planet. "*...You are fighting for...something about liberty, something about liberating a population of people.*"

Liberation seemed to be the theme of the day. So was my soul a Haitian slave, a Black soldier in the Civil War, or an American Indian in South Dakota?

Yikes. It suddenly dawned on me. All the clues might be pointing to *several* lifetimes. Bloody hell.

On my way home from Idaho, we drove through Montana and I was hyper-vigilant to look for clues. At a gas station, I saw a sign that read, "Custer's Last Stand."

"Hubby, o' wise one, who got an A+ in American History, what happened with Custer?"

He told me how Indians had ambushed the famous general at the Battle of Little Big Horn and everyone in Custer's group was killed.

Was this a clue? Maybe it was a *sign* that I was close to a clue and the Universe was nudging me. "You're getting warmer."

I sensed something in the convenience store needed my attention. What could it be? A delicious Slim Jim? Sniff, sniff. The tourist racks looked rather mundane, just brochures of Montana. So I left the shop and waited in the car with my kids for hubby to return. But a voice in my head said, "Go *back* into the store. There's a message there for you." Alrighty then.

So, back into the store I went, and sure enough, all the way to the back, past the numerous tourist racks, was a pile of paper visitor guides to the state of *South Dakota*. I tingled all over.

While my husband continued driving, I looked at the South Dakota map in the brochure. There, as big as life, was the *Missouri* river going through the state. Whoa. Though the

Missouri in my dream had referred to the state, had my subconscious provided *two* clues with the one word? How tricky! I'd read that our subconscious loves metaphor and double entendre. Mine certainly seemed to dig it.

I traced the river's path across the map. It entered South Dakota in the *southeast* corner. I pinched myself. That old TBIF "Colorado" song included the words *south, east, river*...and *clue!* Do you remember which Tarot card highlighted the song? The 3 of Wands. It features a guy wearing a checkerboard cloak standing on a *mountain* looking out at a *river.*

When I had asked the Tarot cards at the beginning of my Idaho trip where one of my significant past lives had taken place, the 8 of Cups and 3 of Wands both featured a river and mountains!

Wands also represent "south." *South* Dakota has lots of mountains, including the one where Mt. Rushmore is carved...and whose face is on it? Abraham Lincoln, the man in my dream with 1841 and Missouri.

David Bengston, the author who believes that John Lennon was John Wilkes Booth, also claims that Lennon has always had an affinity for South Dakota and actually wanted to live there. I have no idea if Mr. Lennon shot Abe Lincoln in another lifetime, but Lennon was shot in front of his apartment building—*The Dakota*—named after the Dakota Territory. A figure of a Dakota Indian keeps watch at the main entrance. Spooky.

Suddenly, my cell phone rang. It was Rod Sterling. "You're traveling through another dimension," he said. "Your next stop: The Twilight Zone."

Life may feel helter skelter, but synchronicity was the Universe gently guiding me. *Pay attention to the clues.* They would provide answers to my far-out rock 'n' roll past-life questions when the Divine Timing was right.

CHAPTER 20

"DR. ROBERT"

—The Beatles

"Artists reflect the collective unconscious and thus give voice to the people. They are not self-professed heroes, but by the very nature of being artists, they are channels from the collective unconscious, and in their quest to create, heroes."[53]
—Jenny Boyd, Ph.D., author

Hot on the trail of synchronicities, with the *Twilight Zone* theme song ringing in my ear, a previous clue resurfaced…and took me on a major detour away from the Civil War, Haiti, and American Indians. The detour was a little book called *The DaVinci Code.*

As mentioned in chapter one, before the TBIF concert in 1998, the initials of the band members' first names had raced through my mind until the letters transformed into the name *Robert.* Who the bleep was Robert? Robert E. Lee? Not even close.

For years, this name perplexed me, but it wasn't until I began investigating alchemy that one particular seventeenth-century *Robert* made my heart skip a few beats. While reading about the **music of the spheres** and alchemy, *this* Robert had often shown up, along with a tingle-tingle sensation, an intuitive nudge. However, I had been ignoring my intuition's pokes for months. Then the name showed up again…in *The DaVinci Code.*

Every mystery novel offers clues and codes. *The DaVinci Code* specifically uses **anagrams**, **acronyms**, and double entendres throughout. The characters of the *The DaVinci Code* discuss the **Divine Feminine, Sacred Geometry, Secret Brotherhoods,** and the **Holy Grail,** among many other esoteric subjects. This is the kind of stuff the Ancient Mystery Schools thrived on. Mysteries, secrets, and clues—just my cup of decaffeinated green tea.

My eyes riveted to a passage that listed the **Grand Masters of the Priory of Sion.** Two names practically leapt off the parchment and kissed me. **Nicholas Flammel,** a real, dead person, considered one of the forefathers of alchemy. Harry Potter fans may recall Nick from J.K. Rowling's first book, *Harry Potter and the Sorcerer's Stone.*

The second name that glowed was the sixteenth person on the list. It was Robert... **Robert Fludd.** He was an alchemist AND into music—the **harmony of the spheres.** A huge tingle-tingle poked me. "PAY ATTENTION THIS TIME!" So, I asked JC and the Tarot cards if there was any possible past-life connection between me and Robert Fludd. Oh, boy! It appears there had been a friendship. Also lots of arguing, betrayal, deception, and deep heartache. Yikes.

I researched Dr. Robert Fludd, and this seventeenth-century dead dude totally swept me off my feet. The guy was a real Renaissance man, and he wore nice white puffy shirts! Sometimes considered an early father of Freemasonry, Dr. Fludd was a devoted member of a secret society known as the Rosicrucian Brotherhood.

The Rosicrucians emerged in the early 1600s with three publications that caused immense excitement throughout Europe. These works declared the existence of a *secret brotherhood* of alchemists and sages who were preparing to transform the arts, sciences, religion, and political and intellectual landscapes of Europe while wars of politics and religion were ravaging the continent.[54]

Although a traditional physician, Dr. Fludd's beliefs were deeply rooted in the occult traditions of astrology, alchemy, the art of memory, chiromancy (palmistry), physiognomy (face reading), and the Jewish Kabbalah. It was like Fludd and I were Siamese twins separated at birth, but time-warped into two different centuries.

Robert Fludd's "medical practice involved a fair sampling of astrology and faith healing and his forceful and magnetic personality was said to help cure his patients."[55] According to author Joscelyn Goodwin, Fludd was something of a psychic healer, which led to attacks against him by outsiders and the medical establishment for being an evil magician. Did someone say magician? Remember the Tarot card that flew out of the deck when I asked which of the cards represented TBIF? *The Magician.*

Keep in mind, the occult was popular during the Middle Ages, so Fludd wasn't unique in working with magic. Even Sir Isaac Newton (the gravity dude) reportedly had a huge personal library that included hundreds of volumes on magic and alchemy. For many, magic and alchemy were about spiritual enlightenment—not warts, curses, and spells.

The duality of good and evil plays a significant role in Fludd's writings—dark and light, like TBIF's black-and-white checkerboard. His illustrations and alchemical concepts sparked profound memories for me! As with the Tarot, this all felt VERY familiar. I didn't get into all of the arcane technical terminology, nor do I understand Latin, but the images that Fludd created are astounding.

He wrote extensively and drew incredible illustrations regarding *music* and its connection to the human soul. He considered the entire universe a musical chromatic instrument. The music of the spheres is "produced from impact upon the paths of the planets, which stand as chords or strings, by the cross travel of the sun from note to note, as from planet to planet."[56] Fludd believed that music, color, and language are allied together.[57] His complex illustration, *The Temple of Music,* appears to be a mnemonic device for the rules of music. It includes a *checkerboard* to show the distances between notes of the musical scale (see appendix).

During my Fludd investigation, I was rummaging through a pile of TBIF's CDs, when one screamed out, "Pick ME!" It was the CD with the *witch doctor* on the cover.

The music brought back a flood of memories. This CD must have tickled my eardrums 200 times during my four-hour work commute to and from New York City in the 1980s. It's probably the most disliked album by fans and critics, yet the songs totally hit *my* aural G-spot.

As the title track started playing, my antennae perked up. The chorus began and, seeing as I'm a psychic brick, it took awhile for a ton of bricks to descend upon my cranium. I listened to the tune again and again. Oh, my heavens, how blind could I be? The song is about a doctor who makes people feel good...with music. Wow, even TBIF's guitarist once said, "...our Doctor is the doctor of music. Music should enter your brain. It's sort of like having a healing power, should make you feel good."[53a] Duh! *Doctor* Fludd believed music is a powerful healing force.

Despite this new synchronicity, I still didn't trust my intuition, though. A past life with the alchemist Robert Fludd? Was I nuts? Time for another intuitive reading.

Diana came recommended by my acupuncturist. When she told me to ask a question, out of my big mouth blurted the four names of the guys in the band. But I made no reference to who they are. I only asked if there was any soul connection between them and a person from the past, Dr. Robert Fludd.

"Yeah, there is," she said. "All four of them are connected to the doctor."

"I don't want to infringe on anybody's past-life privacy—"

"Well, actually, *you* are part of it. All of you have been connected with each other in many lifetimes. In that one, *you* were more familiar with the doctor. The two of you worked together in some respect. You were a co-partner." Diana added, "There is a lot of green around both of you. It symbolizes healing of some sort."

"Which of these four men *might* have been Robert Fludd?" I asked, referring to the four band members in TBIF.

With her **pendulum**, she checked each of their names twice, then she got a "yes" swing and said the name of one of the band members. Now, I won't name names, because I can keep *some* things secret. But I will tell you it was the same guy the intuitive Lee had seen as a revolutionary writer in Old England (Fludd was English). And what about that current English musician who thought TBIF could have been fellow Brummies? I wondered. Maybe we were all Brummies a few centuries ago! I smiled like the cat who'd swallowed a canary.

Whether or not I've had a past life with Dr. Robert Fludd, it feels like I'm *entraining* with this dead dude's vibration. He's a kindred spirit. Fludd believed that all things were connected, that personal transformation is the path to enlightenment. He stood by his convictions despite severe criticism. I'm standing by my convictions about rock music and group reincarnation despite severe criticism too. I consider him an etheric mentor, and a guide on my path toward what the alchemists had sought: self-realization.

Many visionaries like Robert Fludd were mocked and ridiculed because they saw things differently than the status quo. Throughout history, thousands of people in science, medicine, the arts, and politics have been ostracized for their nonconformist ideas. What if our current scientific beliefs and paradigms are barking up the wrong tree? It wouldn't be the first time. (We all know the earth is flat, right?)

Maybe we can't physically prove that God or an afterlife exists because God isn't a concept, but a state of consciousness. Raise our consciousness and God is suddenly everywhere, in all things. Perhaps we must look inward, not outward, to discover God. Wouldn't it be a shock if God is a state of mind?

The Dr. Fludds of this world attempt to integrate two paradoxical universes of matter and spirit, via science and music, because they see everything as the essence of God. The Renaissance alchemists felt that man is full of contradictions and warring passions; that because we exist in a dualistic world, the constant pull of opposites (good vs. evil, masculine vs. feminine) drives us nuts. They understood that to stop this incessant cycle of inner conflict, we need to transform our consciousness…and become one with God.

The alchemists viewed the **Divine Feminine** as a higher path to consciousness. Since we're all born either male or female, they believed it was necessary to balance the opposite sex energy within us for inner harmony, that we need the feminine (and vice-versa) in order to be spiritually complete. To me, the Divine Feminine represents the unseen (spirit, intuition, nurturing, caring, emotions, mystery); whereas, the masculine principle often brings logic, intellect, and reason into the world, which creates physical manifestation. The feminine senses and feels; the masculine thinks and acts.

An ancient alchemical text, *The Chemical Wedding*,*** reflects the need for spiritual union. "The marriage of spirit and soul, [also referred to as] sulfur and quicksilver, sun and moon,

***I mentioned earlier there were three Rosicrucian manifestos; **The Chemical Wedding** is the third manifesto. According to Sharon M.W. from "The Alchemy Website," Robert Fludd greatly admired and was in sympathy to the ideals and intent expressed in the manifestos. He wrote several works to express this admiration and became known as a Rosicrucian Apologist.

or king and queen, is the central symbol of alchemy. Alchemy is based on the view that man…is divided within himself."[58]

This concept of spiritual marriage had appeared in a dream I recorded in 1999, long before reading about alchemy. The lead singer of TBIF was wearing a *red* tank top, and two women were donning *white* wedding gowns. One woman yelled that she couldn't believe the other woman, her sister, had slept with her husband (the singer). In *The Chemical Wedding*, the masculine principle is represented as a Red King; and the feminine, the White Queen. Apparently, my subconscious digs alchemical weddings too!

All this talk of weddings made me wonder if Dr. Fludd had been married. The answer is no. Joscelyn Godwin wrote in his book, *Robert Fludd*, that Fludd had prided himself on "having always remained an 'unstained virgin.' [He] had little sympathy for the frailties of the flesh, and sexual desire figured in his philosophy as the very cause of man's Fall."[59]

Well, *ick*. This lovely phrase about chicks being the downfall of the human race was indelibly etched into my brain. How could my mentor feel so yucky about women? The ancient alchemists knew that *hu*mans are not spiritually complete without the Divine Feminine, but Dr. Fludd felt women are temptation, the devil incarnate, yada yada yada.

I did eventually read that nature, mother earth, was Fludd's mistress and he considered the Divine Feminine to be God's spouse. Those Renaissance dudes were brilliant, but also kinda weird.

Something else kinda weird happened to me during this part of my journey down the Rock 'n' Roll Yellow Brick Road. When writing about Fludd and the Divine Feminine, at times an intense sorrow would blanket my heart. I would suddenly start sobbing and snotting all over my keyboard. *Why, why, why did Dr. Fludd make me cry, cry, cry?*

I asked myself what caused this emotional anguish...and heard, "Meggie's Dead," the phrase from my bizarre dream with the song "Helter Skelter."

Did this mean I had been Meggie in another lifetime, possibly with Dr. Fludd? It seemed that way at first. But then something important dawned on me. The dream had occurred in Idaho shortly after reading Richard Chamberlain's memoir in which he recounts playing Father Ralph in the mini-series, *The Thorn Birds*. Father Ralph could not have the two things he loved most: God *and* the woman he adored, *Meggie*. A-Ha!

Catholic priests are not allowed to marry or make love to a woman. Priests are "unstained virgins." Father Ralph was an unstained virgin (until Meggie stained him halfway through the story)...and so was Dr. Fludd. Had I been attracted to Fludd and he'd rejected me simply because I was a female?

What was this synchronicity telling me? Think, think, think. My relationship with men in this lifetime? Uh oh. I noticed an interesting pattern. My father had rarely discussed God with me, and I had considered him nonreligious, perhaps an atheist. My husband, pretty much the same. TBIF? No idea, though their song lyrics seem secular to me. Philosophically, they certainly are not U2.

Oh, my heavens. Now I understand the meaning of the dream. My subconscious was poking at me: Meggie was a metaphor for the *Divine Feminine*. As a female writing about God and spirituality, the singer in the dream had sung "Meggie's dead" because the men in my world don't believe the metaphysical exists. In other words, "God's dead."

Perhaps Dr. Fludd brought up feelings of sadness because, deep down, I feared that men (including TBIF) would reject me because of my spiritual beliefs and not take me seriously; that I was a fraud, a joke—since science, not intuition, rules. Yet men with whom I *could* share my spiritual insights, such as Dr. Fludd, pushed women aside.

So, as the intuitive at Psychic Horizons noted, I'd *never* been accepted into the brotherhood because of my gender. Just great. Most guys not only had shied away from me because of my intimidating height, now they screamed, "Get lost!—woo-woo, new-agey freak!" Seemed a tall, spiritual gal just couldn't win.

The intuitive Lee had seen that I needed to heal a relationship with a revolutionary writer in old England. Diana had identified Fludd as the same guy, and saw green healing energy around him and me. Even the Tarot cards had indicated a painful emotional connection with Fludd. The message was consistent: I needed to resolve my feelings of rejection with the band, and dudes, in general. Bloody hell.

Apparently I had a few more inner-goobers to heal. Just call me Sleeping Beauty, alchemical metaphor of the Divine Feminine, snoozing away, needing to **wake the bleep up!**

CHAPTER 21

"CRACK THE CODE"

—311

"I believe in the collective unconscious. I believe writing is tapping into that; I believe it's in the air. The good days are really spiritual; you feel that you have tapped into something universal."[60] —Don Henley, musician

My fascination with alchemy was an important clue because alchemists and secret societies used symbols to camouflage their writings and drawings. As archetypes, symbols show up in dreams as metaphors, which is the language of the subconscious. Carl Jung had discovered this phenomenon as well, when he studied alchemy. He noticed that correlations between alchemical symbols and the images his patients related to him from their dreams were often one and the same. That's how he came to coin the term **collective unconscious.**

While I was snoring away in my unenlightened state, the number *four* began bubbling up from my subconscious again. Four, four, four? It must be a significant clue. So I pried my eyes open. What did Sleeping Beauty see? Four numbers—11:11.

Yes, those digits from chapter 15, which represent an encoded *wake-up call* to remind us of our mission in life. I had already figured out there are *four* suits in the Tarot, and four members in most rock bands. And now, lo and behold, I discovered that four is considered the number of the universe! Four elements (earth, air, fire, and water), four seasons, four states of matter, four directions. *Four, four, four.*

Four is also a favorite among Rosicrucians and alchemists. I kid you not. The Rosicrucians had a symbolic cross (called the Rosy Cross) with *four* points, representing the *four* directions. The horizontal part of the cross represents east to west and our physical experience; the vertical, north to south, symbolizes our spiritual awareness.

While we're on numbers, 22 also wins a popularity contest, because in numerology, it connects to 4 (2+2). There are 22 tiny petals in the rose of the Rosy Cross and 22 cards in the Major Arcana (the Tarot was highly influenced by the Rosicrucians). My twisted mind also links TBIF's 22 album titles with all of the Major Arcana!

And there's more to four. Physically, all *hu*man beings are a combination of *four* things. In 1953, the smarty-pants scientists James Watson and Francis Crick discovered the double helix and the *four* DNA bases that make up all living things: cytosine, adenine, thymine, and guanine (CATG).

Why had the number four constantly been racking my brain? Because, God is a four-letter word. Come to find out, four is the number of the **Tetragrammaton**. In Hebrew, the Tegragrammaton represents the name of God, symbolized in the four letters YHVH (say it with me: yod-hay-vav-hay). God=YHVH.

YHVH is a code. According to Tarot expert Rachel Pollack, "In the writings of the Kabbalists, the letters YHVH do not form a name in the sense of a person, *but rather they depict a formula that is the process of creation.*"[61]

Author and scientist Greg Braden cracked this formula in his groundbreaking book, *The God Code*. This great work had pleaded with me to take it home when I was perusing a metaphysical bookstore. I'm a sucker for begging books and it's a good thing, because Braden makes a strong case that the letters YHVH

(God) can be connected to the *four* base pairs of our DNA (cytosine, adenine, thymine, and guanine) through the atomic weight of primary elements. Braden also gets into alchemy and the four elements of air, water, earth, and fire and their symbolic meanings in Hebrew.

To make a long story short: by connecting the four DNA bases (CATG) to the four elements and the four Hebrew letters YHVH, we get the message "God/Eternal within the body."[62] So God is literally encoded in each *human* being! It's right in our DNA. *We* are God. Co-creators with the Big Cheese. How's that for my soul slamming me with numero quatro?

Guess what? The letters YHVH were widely used by Robert Fludd in his writings, too. Not only that, Rosicrucians and alchemists were also code and number freaks. They loved hidden messages and symbolism, such as **chronograms**, in their works.

A chronogram is a sentence or inscription in which specific letters, interpreted as numerals, stand for a particular date when rearranged. In 1617, a book by Robert Fludd was published with the date hidden in a chronogram on the cover within the Latin words ChrIstVs MVnDo VIta, meaning "Christ, life to the world." The savvy reader can solve the chronogram by reordering the capitals in the words CIVMVDVI to MDCVVVII—the Roman numerals for the year 1617. Tricky hidden stuff!

While chronograms use letters as a secret code, and archetypal symbols contain secret codes for our unconscious mind, it seems codes apparently come in many forms. Even in a rock song's lyrics. I pointed out the title of a TBIF song to an intuitive, non-fan friend, saying "What do you think of this?"

After a moment, she exclaimed, "Oh, my gosh. It's a hidden code!"

Ya got that right, girlfriend. The letters represent the opening notes/chords of the song. Here's an anagram of the song title: *faced*. Have fun. It's a bit tricky to figure out.

The lead guitarist in TBIF is a total word trickster. He's been called *The King of Double Entendre,* because his lyrics have numerous meanings. Many of their song titles contain a play on words. For decades, fans have argued over the possible hidden meanings in lyrics, album covers, and inside jackets. It's a code-fest for those into this stuff. No wonder I love TBIF's music. Like attracts like!

Another famous code that the alchemists used (e.g., Dr. Fludd, DaVinci) was the **pentagram** (five pointed star inside in a circle). This symbol of *protection* represents spirit infused into man. The upward point of the star represents spirit; the other four points symbolize the elements earth, air, fire, and water. Man = God.

Don't go having a hissy fit about the pentagram because someone told you it's the symbol of devil worshippers. From what I've read, only the inverted pentagram, when the point of the star is downward, is used to conjure up the powers of evil. Interesting how the same symbol, when turned in a different direction, has a completely opposite meaning.

There are other reasons that fraternal societies, like the Rosicrucian Brotherhood, used secret numbers, codes, and symbols. These groups were clandestine not because they were snotty supremacists, but because their ideas were radical. They went against the mainstream and they didn't want to get chopped into tiny bits by the Church for heresy. If I were a Rosicrucian in the seventeenth century, I'd have hid under my bed, too.

It amazes me that even in today's society, I still need to hide. When I once told some folks I kept hearing the words *archetype* and *four* in my head, I truly thought they would summon the men with the white jacket. But what if this isn't insanity? What if it is the soul's way of communicating important clues about music, nature, and the consciousness of humankind?

So, can I please emerge from under my bed without the fear of everyone chopping me up into tiny bits in this lifetime? I really want to escape those annoying dust bunnies. Just say the secret code-word, and I'll come out. What is it? Here's a hint or a clue. It has to do with the four initials of the guys in TBIF.

CHAPTER 22

"HE AIN'T HEAVY, HE'S MY BROTHER"

—Bobby Scott and Bob Russell

"Each artist attracts his own different set of fans.... They know it's something unusual and special that they're not going to get anywhere else...young and old, both sexes, all come out. They all look at each other like, Wow, what are those people over there?...They're surprised at their own diversity." [63] —Joe Satriani, guitarist

It's much nicer being a fan, part of a group, and dancing to my favorite rock tunes than shakin' in my boots, alone under my bed. After crawling out of hiding, the initials of the band's first names kept nudging at me. Poke, poke, poke. *Pay attention.*

Their initials had originally triggered the name Robert. Now, when I rearranged the letters, a ton of bricks descended on my poor little head and a new secret code-word emerged. The first or second letters and the middle initial of TBIF's first names precisely spell B-R-O-T-H-E-R. Wow.

Another important clue! But what did it mean?

I came across the following about Robert Fludd and the Rosicrucian *Brotherhood*. Once again, I started snotting all over my keyboard.

The brilliant fire of the Rosicrucian proclamations, and the noble labours of men like Robert Fludd burnt into the consciousness of Europe the idea that there is a Brotherhood of Adepts in the world, striving to disseminate truth to those who spiritually desire and deserve it…. Remaining invisible to the eyes of the world, the Rosicrucians influenced thought and politics in many directions, including helping to found the Royal Society and providing the basis for Freemasonry. The Brotherhood as an ideal and fact has ever since remained as a seed in the mind of humanity. [64]

The word "*brother*hood" stabbed in my left ventricle. It deeply saddens me that the powerful message held by the Renaissance alchemists and Rosicrucians—that each of us can personally follow the path to spiritual enlightenment—receded in the mass consciousness as the scientific revolution gained steam and the **Newtonian model** took over.

Maybe there is hope for us yet. Despite our scientific knowledge and technological advances today, there is a powerful resurgent interest in metaphysics. We are no longer just praying that God exists. We want to KNOW whether or not we truly are spiritual beings.

Brotherhood kept poking me. I vaguely recalled reading about *The Great White Brotherhood* years before when living in England for a semester during college. So I looked it up on the Internet. Oh, my. The Great White Brotherhood refers to the concept of an enlightened community of adepts, on earth and in the hereafter, who have benevolent aims toward the spiritual development of the human race.[65] The word 'White' refers only to the soul's intent, or level of consciousness, as white light refers to the highest level of thinking. It has no connection to either race or snotty white folks' skin color.

The Tarot dudes, Arthur Edward Waite and Aleister Crowley, were involved with a secret group of initiates called the

Hermetic Order of the Golden Dawn, who sought spiritual enlightenment. According to a book on Crowley, the Golden Dawn, which has ties with the Rosicrucians, represented itself to be the visible and earthly outer order of the Great White Brotherhood.

This is too bizarre. My soul led me to alchemy and the Tarot, and the Tarot decks I'd been using were created by guys in a secret brotherhood. TBIF's initials spell b-r-o-t-h-e-r, and the intuitives at Psychic Horizons saw that TBIF and I had some kind of fraternal, *brotherly* connection. We worked with the occult and alchemy, and had to keep things *secret*. Something went awry that we felt guilty about. Believe it or not, this is a Rosicrucian *brotherhood* maxim: *To know, to will, to dare, and to keep silent.*

As mentioned earlier, Crowley is on the cover of a Beatles album, and several other rock musicians were interested in the guy. Hey, wouldn't rock 'n' roll be considered a male fraternity, a *brotherhood* of dudes united with a common purpose? Rock musicians fascinated with the occult? The parallels are making my stomach do the funky twist-knotty dance. Bloody HELLLP!

It's all too much for my heart to handle. What's happening to me? I no longer know who I am. Living in two centuries causes a major case of schizophrenia. Am I a typical, stay-at-home mom in Colorado who digs rock music, or a member of the freakin' Rosicrucian Brotherhood during the Renaissance? Was I trying to awaken society with a bunch of dudes who are presently rock stars? You can lock me up and I'll throw the damn key away myself.

Danae had said that I wanted to complete something in this lifetime with the soul of a guy in TBIF. Is this book a part of finishing up what we started centuries ago, and will it make amends for something that went awry? But I've never met my brothers in this lifetime. I'm going solo. All I have is their music, and watching them perform on stage, to help me figure it all out.

When the woman at the Boulder TBIF concert (the show where I had intuitives planted in the audience) asked, "Is your brother still here?" (meaning the singer), the Universe was sending me a major message and I was too dense to know it. Psychic brick here, pointing finger at self.

My response, "I don't have a brother," was a powerful metaphor of my identity. I am an only child…and a woman trying to spiritually wake up a male fraternity, a brotherhood, of musicians. But my brothers don't seem to hear the 11:11 alarm ringing yet. They've hit the snooze button, and remain warmly tucked in bed. *They're* Sleeping Beauty. For now, I'm all alone in my quest. Bloody hell.

Oh brother. Now look what Mr. Whiskers dragged in from the Internet. The Hebrew definition of *brother* is "the one that acts as a barrier to *protect* the family." Protect? As mentioned earlier, the pentagram is a symbol of spiritual *protection*, and was widely used by Rosicrucians and alchemists. This got me thinking. If TBIF's initials spell the word *brother*, and some brotherhoods focus on spirituality and enlightenment—and rock music is a brotherhood—are rock musicians spiritually protecting something?

The word brother and its Hebrew meaning, protection, kept nudging at me BIG TIME. So, I asked the Tarot (and JC) "What's rock music protecting?" I intuitively pulled four cards.

One card in the spread, the Ace of Cups (represents love and unity), contains symbols of the *brotherhood* of mankind. An important clue! But I couldn't piece it all together. Damn. *Patience, Grasshopper.*

Zen Master ain't my middle name. However, learning to live fully in the present—knowing that all things unfold according to a master Divine Timing plan—is part of Grasshopper's journey.

Hopping forward I became obsessed with receiving the

answer hidden in those four Tarot cards. Over and over, I questioned, what were rock musicians protecting? Ask and it is given.

While pondering this imponderable, I went to the park with my two young daughters, now ages three and five. As they giggled on the swings, a boy came over to play with them, away from his group on the baseball field. He was much older, about twelve, and developmentally challenged.

My daughters went down the slide with the boy several times. I sensed I needed to closely watch them. Suddenly, I saw him holding my five-year-old upside down, with her head just inches above the ground. I hollered at him to put her down gently, and he dropped her like a hot potato. She was fine. I was not.

The next thing I know, he's pulling on the legs of my three-year-old as she is climbing up the slide's metal steps. I screamed, "Let go of her legs!" I safely got her down.

Soon after, a chaperone came over and said to the boy, "Michael, it's time to go home." Michael waltzed away as if nothing had happened.

I sat on the bench, amazed. I may not be a member of a *brotherhood*, but I am a member of motherhood and we protect our own, too.

The next morning, the name *Michael* kept nudging at me. I was taking a shower, with soap in my hair. "All right, JC. Who the heck is Michael?"

Louder than a Who rock concert, I heard: *Archangel Michael.*

"Archangel Michael? What's he got to do with anything?"

Good Grief, Charlie Brown. My research indicated that Michael is the leader of all the Archangels...and in charge of *protection,* courage, strength, truth, and integrity. Prayers to him reflect a wish for protection. *Michael* is the big kahuna in the angel realm, and oversees the protection of the human race. He's like our big *Brother*. I sat at my computer in total disbelief. No bleeping way.

And get this—Archangel Michael was a favorite of Dr. Fludd.

CHAPTER 23

"TALKIN' WORLD WAR III BLUES"

—Bob Dylan

"…They prove that not conceptual speech, but music rather, is the element through which we are best spoken to by mystical truth. Many mystical scriptures are indeed little more than musical compositions."[66]

—William James, twentieth-century philosopher

Diana, the intuitive, said something earlier that weaved together numbers, symbols, secret societies, brotherhoods, and music. I had asked why the group-soul reincarnation theme was so strong for me.

"Now, please don't take this the wrong way," she said, "but I see a swastika. I don't know what that means for you."

Swastika??? I was connected to alchemists and Voodoo, now the Nazis? Bloody hell.

But not necessarily. An important experience several months before reminded me that the swastika symbol has numerous meanings. It's not just about Hitler.

Whew. That's a relief.

It was Halloween night and my friend Shari and her two kids had joined my family for trick-or-treating. When our goblins knocked on one particular door, something shocked me more than seeing ghosts and mini-Frankenstein monsters wandering through my neighborhood. On the doorsill were three little swastikas in a row. I looked again. Sure enough. There they were.

An East Indian woman answered the door, wearing a sari. Since my neighborhood was ethnically diverse, and my friend Shari was Jewish, I was appalled to think someone had put anti-Semitic symbols on a neighbor's home.

We thanked the Indian woman for the treats. As Shari and I walked across the street, I asked her, "Did you see the symbols on the doorsill?"

She smiled. "Yes, but the swastika was going in the *opposite* direction of the Nazi symbol. It's used by Indians for good luck."

How did Shari know this? Her husband is of East Indian descent.

If I hadn't had that conversation with Shari prior to my reading with Diana, my freak-out level would have been off the Richter scale.

Tidbits on the origins of the swastika: The symbol represents good luck and being happy. The image symbolizes the *four* directions and *four* seasons flowing harmoniously as the natural order of the world. More *four*. More importantly, the swastika stands for circular movement and *rebirth* and sometimes represents the concept of reincarnation.

Symbols don't exist merely to make pottery look pretty. They have been an integral element in *hu*man designs for millennia—because they carry energy and intent, and communicate with our subconscious mind.

The swastika is a sacred symbol of many religions including Hinduism, Buddhism, Jainism, and the Hopi and Navajo American Indians. But guess who else was into the swastika symbol? Yep. My alchemical brothers. According to the website, *Full Moon Paradise*:

> To the alchemists, the swastika represents the two principle energies that act in the world: Electrical (upright

bar) and Magnetic (horizontal bar). These energies—like all energies—are dynamic and are thus represented as being in motion. Were the swastika to spin quickly enough, it would become a circle. One of the goals of the alchemists is to symbolically turn the swastika into a circle: To turn the divergent energies of the world into something truly infinite.[67]

Sacred geometry and numerology both demonstrate how numbers, symbols, and letters manifest according to a vibrational code—as do all things. The ancient alchemists sought to transform our physical form into light, so we could realize our oneness with God.

In contrast, Hitler's swastika carried the energy of hate and separation. Instead of honoring how all beings are aspects of God(dess), or the One, he and millions of others agreed that separation, division, and hierarchy are the true nature of reality. Big fat liar! Such elitism and arrogance are manifestations of the ego-shadow, the false self.

Sadly, science, too, has had its periods where it focused on separation. For eons, systematic knowledge of the physical and material world was gained through observation and experimentation. In western society, science zeroed in on reductionism, to see how small things got, and wanted to discover the teeniest particle in the universe. At first, all particles seemed to be separate from one another.

Then **quantum physicists** came along early in the twentieth century and freaked everyone out. "Excuse us—but, oops! Science has got a bunch of stuff wrong." They discovered that everything at the subatomic level is somehow connected. This suggested a *unity* among even the smallest known particles in the physical world: that you and I are made of a bunch of particles...and that we are connected at an imperceptible level.

I began to see a pattern. My ego-shadow saw my thoughts and body as separate from everything else. But my soul kept pushing me toward understanding that everything is one. Which was true? Could *both* perspectives be valid because truth is not absolute, and fluctuates depending upon one's level of consciousness? If we raise our consciousness, does our perspective shift from separateness to unity?

My research led to an unexpected find. Hitler supposedly studied esoteric scriptures in Vienna to find out more about certain secret teachings. Several websites mention that Hitler also believed in group reincarnation.

Group Reincarnation? Chills shot up and down my spine. This couldn't be possible.

The swastika is a symbol of rebirth, and group reincarnation books revolve around a theme of oppression and trauma, often genocide. Hitler's regime was perhaps the most abhorrent extreme of ethnic cleansing the modern world has seen. He showed us what can happen when our ego demands control. He acted out darkness and was the antithesis of the *brotherhood* of mankind.

The esoteric information that Hitler allegedly came across was intended to show the path toward enlightenment and unity with God. Yet that same information, used with the intent to harm instead of heal, caused destruction and horror for millions.

I desperately wanted to understand if there were connections among the Ancient Mystery Schools, Rosicrucians, alchemists, and Hitler. Had Fludd and other members of the Brotherhood sensed that if their codes and messages fell into the hands of darkness, devastation would ensue? Had they kept everything a secret to protect us?

Since the word *brother* in Hebrew means "one who protects"

and I'd been led to Hitler and the Jews via the swastika, the sig-
nificance of the synchronicity of protecting my daughters from
the boy named Michael was becoming clearer. Obviously, it was
crucial that I make an important association to Archangel
Michael.

Michael is generally presented as the field commander of
the Army of God. According to rabbinic Jewish tradition, this
angel acted as an advocate of Israel.[68] Legend has it Mike's army
kicked Satan's butt and drove his posse of evil angels out of heav-
en. Good won over evil.

But the theme of all group reincarnation books is the opposite: evil over good, causing oppression and trauma. Jews, black
slaves, and American Indians have all had an overwhelming share
of oppression.

Somehow, during my group-reincarnation research phase, I
had missed an important book, *Beyond the Ashes: Cases of
Reincarnation from the Holocaust,* by Rabbi Gershom. I discovered online reviews in which the rabbi analyzes a dozen case his-
tories of people's vivid and horrific memories of past lives during
the Holocaust. Their memories appear to have caused unusual
phobias and unique physical symptoms in their new present lifetimes.

Many people the rabbi counseled were born shortly after
the war in the 1940s and 1950s. I was born in 1963, and have
always wondered about my childhood phobias of death, war, and
mass annihilation. After discovering my possible soul connection
with alchemy and the swastika, I couldn't help but question if I
had lived during WWII and experienced the horrors of the
Holocaust.

But why would a large group of souls choose such a painful
and traumatic lifetime? I can't answer that. I only know that each
lifetime fits our soul's plan for our overall growth and experience

over the course of *many* incarnations. Our soul understands the bigger picture of *all* our lives. It's hard to realize the broader scope of our life purpose if we have a myopic view and believe we live only one life.

Perhaps millions of souls incarnated during World War II knowing that their destruction would eventually raise the consciousness of others in order to send a message to humanity that love and acceptance must be the highest ideals; otherwise, we will ultimately destroy ourselves. Maybe the message from our higher selves is that we've been fighting the wrong enemy for thousands of years. Is the bad guy not another person or group, but our own ego, our shadow, because it perceives everything as separate?

So, how do we heal our individual and collective or societal *shadow*? I'm still trying to figure that out. My guess is that we need to accept the dark in order to be truly in the light. In a world comprised of duality, everything has two sides: occult, magic, alchemy, Rosicrucians, Voodoo, and swastikas. Nothing is completely dark or light, bad or good, not even rock music. Rock music can bring us joy, the light; or it can lead us to addiction and physical gratification, the dark. As noted above, our soul chooses which path to explore. In the end, all roads lead to a greater understanding of our Self.

Jimi Hendrix once commented, "In World War II all these countries were completely against each other, complete opposite. Now we're getting them all together, through the idea of music."[69] That makes perfect sense to me. The revolution in rock music during the 1960s promoted peace, not war, and freedom of expression—ideals the antithesis of Hitler's regime. If music has the power to heal and transform, what better way than to surround ourselves with music that resonates from our soul's purpose?

Archangel Michael is a warrior of light. To me, the

Rosicrucian Brotherhood was comprised of warriors of light. Oddly enough, intuitives had told me that TBIF and their fans have been armies of light. So are rock musicians a modern brotherhood bringing healing frequencies to our planet through their music and lyrics in an attempt to raise our mass consciousness? Brotherhood then. Brotherhood now.

Perhaps rock music is such a powerful impetus because it connects us with our inner light, our bliss; and counters feelings of separateness, our ego-shadow. Bliss leads to peace. Peace leads to healing. May each of us find our own light...and heal the world through music.

PART THREE

"Heal Your Heart"

—Steve Miller Band

"Your time is limited, so don't waste it living someone else's life. Don't be trapped by dogma—which is living with the results of other people's thinking. Don't let the noise of other's opinions drown out your own inner voice. And most important, have the courage to follow your heart and intuition. They somehow already know what you truly want to become. Everything else is secondary." —Steve Jobs, Apple co-founder

CHAPTER 24

"SIGN LANGUAGE"

—Eric Clapton

"I think I should have no other mortal wants, if I could always have plenty of music. It seems to infuse strength into my limbs and ideas into my brain. Life seems to go on without effort, when I am filled with music."

—George Eliot, pen name for Mary Ann Evans, Victorian era English novelist

At this juncture, several pieces of the reincarnation puzzle started to fall into place. Unconscious memories of other lifetimes seemed to be influencing my present fears, as well as explaining why I was drawn to certain unusual subjects, like alchemy. Most surprising to me was the puzzle piece about me being a writer in other lifetimes. Besides the intuitive Lee and the palm reader emphasizing my love for the written word, several years ago another clairvoyant saw me in the fifteenth century taking a "brave and bold stance in my writing." These psychic readings helped me find a part of myself of which I hadn't been aware, and now writing was becoming a gratifying obsession.

Attending TBIF concerts was also an obsession. I needed my fix and, fortunately, they would perform in Denver in a few weeks, touring with the alternative rock band Cake. With so much behind me, I could hardly wait to see the band again.

Then my intuition nudged me. A part of me desperately wanted to let TBIF know I was on this wild, wacky journey of self-discovery through their music, but how do you send such an unusual message to an unattainable rock band?

A well-adjusted person might hang out near their tour bus and try to catch them after a concert. Such a bold idea sounded fantabulous, but the thought of personally meeting them to let them know that I believed we had past lives together gave me that funky knot in my stomach. We all know how rock stars feel about stalkers and weirdoes obsessed with reincarnation.

So, how could shy Superfan Girl communicate with the band? Think, think, think.

I've got it! I'm a *writer*. I'll make a sign!

It was a general admission show, so I'd be able to get up close to the stage and they could read my *written* message. So much more comfy than face-to-face.

What should the sign say? I wondered. How about, "Haven't We Met Before? During the Civil War?" Or "Alchemists Do It Better." Or my favorite, "Past Lives Rock!" Nope. Too bold and too shocking, even for rock stars who have seen and heard it all.

A less alarming phrase finally popped into my noggin: *I Found all the Parts to My Soul through the Healing Power of TBIF's Music.*

Fantabulous! Totally noninvasive.

Only one problem: I would have to hold up the sign. Pass the Rolaids.

I decided to stop being a lily-livered sissy, and I created a masterpiece even Michelangelo would have been proud of. My sign had big black letters printed off the computer, the words "Soul" and "Healing Power" in red, all glued onto two large white pieces of poster board. Down each side, alternating black squares created TBIF's black-and-white checkerboard motif.

Several days later at an Abraham gathering of spiritually hip friends, I unveiled my sign and asked for feedback. Everyone got the drift that it terrified me to show the band my message. Two women were excited to give me moral support and offered to attend the concert with me. So there was no backing out. I was obligated to go through with it. I really wanted to. I just kept getting that funky Voodoo knot in my stomach.

Everyone at the Abraham gathering assured me that the sign didn't push the envelope. Nevertheless, when the morning of the concert arrived, I was more nervous than on my wedding day. I compulsively thought about the band's reaction. Would they hate it? Would they find it weird? What would the guitarist say, if anything? TBIF's concerts always brought me joy, but this....

This girl with the sparkly hat needed a major pacifier. I ran to my Tarot deck for guidance and comfort. I started to ask the cards how the band would react to my sign, and WHACK, my soul slapped me upside the head.

It's not about the band, Laura. It's about making a small statement as to who you are. It's about facing your fears from the past. Stop projecting the future. Live in the NOW!

Whoa. Another major lesson.

So, if I had only made the sign for a positive reaction from the band, I shouldn't take it at all. I musn't be attached to the guitarist's or anyone else's response. Their acknowledgement didn't matter one iota.

I understood this intellectually, but my ego-shadow was still triggered in a major way. To find my balance, I used the vowel mantras for a few minutes and envisioned pushing fear out of my body with each exhaled tone. That softened things a bit.

I then asked the Universe for healing, took a few deep breaths, and devoted several moments to imagining myself holding up the sign...with a smile on my face. Since the Law of Attraction states that like attracts like, if I embodied happy, happy, joy, joy, TBIF would receive a warm, fuzzy vibe.

Then it hit me. Positive energy was even more important to

send to the band than the message on the sign, because music is all about emotions and vibrations.

I then found myself being able to let go, truly let go, and I started to feel excited. What more surprises might be in store for me?

I pulled the Tao Oracle card GRACE and got a surprising message: To be a true star is to radiate well-being and an attitude that says, "I feel at home with myself and with the world."[70] A woman's outer beauty is a reflection of her inner grace.

When it was time to leave for the concert, I was free of needing the band's approval. I took my poster, all rolled up with hot-pink rubber bands. Very classy. Just call me Grace.

While standing in line outside the venue, I chatted with several young whippersnappers who were there to see the band Cake. What a rude awakening. My ancient ass was old enough to be the mother of just about everyone around me. Older but wiser, right?

Inside, first thing, I trotted to the powder room with another TBIF fan. My huge rolled-up poster felt like a flashing neon advertising: "I'm a past-life Superfreak!"

The fan asked what it said, and I told her. Would tomatoes fall from the sky? She simply remarked "Oh, that's nice" and walked away. I breathed a huge sigh of relief.

Then I scoped out the theater. It was standing room only, and only a handful of fans were near the stage. I spotted a TBIF fan I'd met at a Winter Park, Colorado concert a few months before. While shooting the breeze with her I got a "that's cool" reaction about the sign. Even her husband commented, "A life without introspection is a life not worth living."

Whew! I profusely thanked the Universe for these little encouraging *signs.*

My spiritually hip amigos, Leslie and Rochelle, arrived midway through one of the warm-up acts. During the break before TBIF took the stage, my pals reassured me that I would not expire if I held up my sign, and they promised to fend off any projectile tomatoes. What are friends for?

When TBIF finally graced us with their presence, I took off the rubber bands and waited for the right moment.

Okay, there was the guitarist, doing his shtick with the audience. Wait, wait, wait. Not yet. He's walking around and nodding to some people near his side of the stage. Wait, wait, wait. Not yet. Oh, there's the singer and bass player, right in front of me. Wait, wait, wait. Not yet. What insane person said patience is a virtue? Smack them for me. Oh, oh, oh, here he comes. The guitarist strolled toward my side of the stage. Now, now, now!

UP, UP, UP went my arms, with my super-sized poster in front of me, totally obstructing my view. Uh oh. I'm not Superman. I can't see through oak tag paper! I turned to Leslie (she's almost six-feet herself) and yelled over the music, "Did he see it? Can I take it down?"

She craned her neck to peer around the sign. Wait, wait, wait. Finally she yelled into my ear, "Okay!"

Hallelujah! My arms were killing me!

She said the guitarist had enough time to read it, and the singer had spied it, too. I beamed with joy, rolled the sign back up, and enjoyed the show.

That is until halfway through the concert when the guitarist announced that there were *two* signs in the audience he wanted to acknowledge. Oh, for the love of God. I had to go through this again?

Wait, wait wait. Not yet. He was reading the other woman's sign. It was her 112th TBIF show. Wait, wait, wait. Not yet. He walked to my side of the stage. I quickly pulled off the hot-pink rubber bands and held up the colossal sign.

He read it to the audience. Gulp. I was so nervous that my brain oozed out of my ears. I had absolutely no freakin' idea what he said. Something about body parts. Must be in reference to the I Found all the Parts on the sign, I figured. I grinned like the Cheshire Cat. My brothers had got the message.

Despite my initial doubt, my soul had urged me to express myself. *Go ahead. Take a chance.* So, I had.

> And what happened then…?
> Well…in Rock 'n' Rollville they say
> That Laura's small soul
> Grew three sizes that day!

My soul got a medal of honor for facing my fear. Whether lifetimes as a black soldier, a fighter for the light on another planet, or a Rosicrucian during the Renaissance, tonight this spiritual warrior had prevailed…and I was tomato-free!

But I was about to need a vat of metaphysical Alka-Seltzer.

CHAPTER 25
"VOODOO CHILE BLUES"

—Jimi Hendrix

"I think music in itself is healing. It's an explosive expression of humanity. It's something we are all touched by. No matter what culture we're from, everyone loves music."[71]

—Billy Joel, musician

Reflecting on the concert, I realized that my journey was more about facing my fears than focusing on reincarnation. Maybe it was time to ditch the idea of uncovering past lives with the band and fans, and move on?

Yet I had come so far! I whined. All of the previous synchronicities indicated that a mammoth past-life discovery was right around the corner. If only I would turn into a Beagle and keep on digging!

The corner this hound dog turned was back into Voodoo, for some god-awful reason. I could have explored American Indians, Civil War soldiers, or alchemy—but Haiti and Voodoo pulled me totally off course, as if into the freaky Bermuda Triangle.

In the midst of this bizarre obsession, I wrote to several authorities on Voodoo, asking if a checkerboard image was used in any of their ceremonies, or if Voodoo had any known association to alchemy. The response was: a few possible connections to alchemy, nothing significant.

Even though I had read that Voodoo is a sacred religion to the Haitians, whenever I considered the possibility that I had done black magic in another life, that twisty knotty feeling in my gut plagued me. The guilt was overwhelming, and I wanted to puke.

These darker feelings were corroborated by Carolyn, an intuitive who had hoped to attend the Boulder show back in April for my research, but couldn't make it. She'd come highly recommended and had recently completed **Barbara Brennan's energy healing program**. So, we got together at a local coffee shop and I brought pictures of the guys in the band. Since she could read energy, I wondered what she'd pick up about them.

Her impressions centered more on *me*. She said that when I talked about TBIF, my energy got pretty wacky, diffusing out into the ethers. A healthy vibrational field around a person's body is stronger and more contained, like a glowing light six inches all around. My vibration was splayed all over and lost power as it moved outward. She said I wasn't using my creative energy very effectively when I spoke about the band and my writing.

Really? What about holding up the sign at the concert and all the synchronicities that had blown me away in Idaho? Weren't these signs I was on the right track?

For the previous two years, nothing but unbelievable enthusiasm and joy had filled my heart on my journey of self-discovery. But as Carolyn's reading pointed out, my synchronistic joyride had turned into the house of horrors when the possibility of a Voodoo lifetime had crossed my Yellow Brick Road. This Voodoo stuff threw me a curve ball I never saw coming.

That's because I didn't pay attention when the Tarot had warned that Magic (the Magician card) had brought me fear and emotional upset (see chapter twelve).

I took a hard look at my mystical experiences and questioned if I was making myself sick over nothing. Was reincarnation even real? Maybe I *was* delusional. But the feeling of dread wouldn't go away. Fear and guilt were triggering my ego-shadow to the point that I sent an urgent S.O.S to God: *Send Help!*

And what did the Big Cheese send back? Another synchronicity. I was walking through my guest bedroom shortly after my request for divine intervention, when I spied a book left behind by a houseguest: *The Seven Spiritual Laws of Success* by Deepak Chopra. It was sitting there all lonely, urging me to pick it up. I did and a *hug* overtook me, which surprised me because I didn't really get Deepak's spiel. His books are about healing and I had nothing to heal—at least not until I'd started this journey down the Rock 'n' Roll Yellow Brick Road.

Unsurprisingly, the book opened at the section "Law of Intention and Desire." This chapter is primarily what Abraham also espouses about the Law of Attraction. Dr. Chopra emphasizes that at the quantum-mechanical level all things are connected and, when we place our attention on something, it grows stronger in our life; that whatever we take our attention away from dwindles and disappears. Our *intention* triggers transformation. What we think about, we bring about.

Abraham says there isn't any law of assertion; there is only the Law of Attraction. The Universe doesn't hear the word NO; it only hears YES. We can shout *no* as loudly as we want; no to drugs, no to the Iraqi war. When we focus on what we *don't* want, that's the vibration of what we bring to ourselves—because we are focused on it. What we resist, persists.

I had tried to follow Abraham's advice and focus on positive, happy thoughts; but Voodoo Girl wasn't anywhere close to being a vibrational match to happy, happy, joy, joy. What if I had done some nasty deeds that had killed or hurt others in a past life? Part of my karma might be to get knocked off in this life. By writing this less-than-mainstream book, what if someone would want to liquidate me? My ego-shadow became utterly paranoid.

The Sanskrit word *karma* translates as *action*. In Buddhism, however, karma mainly refers to our *intention* or motivation when committing an action. Contrary to popular opinion, karma is not good or bad; it's neutral. According to Wikipedia:

> Karma is not about retribution, vengeance, punishment or reward; karma simply deals with what is. The effects of all deeds actively create past, present, and future experiences, thus making one responsible for one's own life, and the pain and joy it brings to others. In religions that incorporate reincarnation, karma extends through one's present life and all past and future lives as well.[72]

A famous rock lyric states that *instant karma's gonna get you*. But sometimes karma isn't so instantaneous. According to David Bengston, many lifetimes may pass before we *choose* to accept our karma. Choose our karma? Because the soul gets the bigger picture of all our lifetimes, it might not be in our best interest to balance our karma in this or even the next life. Before we incarnate, our soul supposedly picks specific unhealed emotional boogers from our previous lifetimes to work through in our upcoming incarnation.

For example, shortly before he was shot, John Lennon, who wrote the song "Instant Karma," reportedly said he felt someone might kill him. If he *was* John Wilkes Booth, perhaps the karma of shooting Abraham Lincoln had leaked from his unconscious? Were my feelings of dread a sign that I was choosing to accept my karma for my past-life actions in this lifetime?

Chopra's little book acted like metaphysical Alka-Seltzer on my gut's fear and guilt. With the third spiritual law, the Law of Karma, Chopra says there are three ways to deal with our karma:

Pay our karmic debts. Often done unconsciously and with a good deal of suffering, because no debt ever goes unpaid.

Transcend our karma through the practice of meditation.

Transmute or transform our karma to a more desirable experience.

One way to transmute our karma is to look at our life's ka-ka from a different perspective. Finding the silver lining in our experiences is the more karmically enlightened path down the Yellow Brick Road. Tired of relationships that bring pain? Never seem to have enough moola? Health or weight ain't what the old gray mare used to be?

Maybe we should ask ourselves, "What is *my* part in creating this mess? Why do I keep attracting blockheads into my life? What are my deeper beliefs about myself that I've never acknowledged or paid attention to?"

When we turn our attention inward and accept responsibility for all of our actions, words, and deeds: *Shift happens.*

Our vibration must first *shift* before we can see a change in our life experiences. Our thoughts and feelings send out subconscious signals to everyone else's vibrational antennae. The people who match that signal and vibration are attracted to it like groupies to a rock star, whether we like it or not.

While doing this transformation of our karma, Chopra says to ask ourselves questions like, "What can I learn from this experience? What is the message the Universe is giving to me? How can I make this experience useful to my fellow human beings? By doing this, you look for the seed of opportunity and then tie that seed of opportunity with your **dharma**, your purpose in life. This allows you to transmute the karma into a new expression."[73]

Chopra gives an example of both karma and dharma with a story about a person who breaks a leg while playing sports. "If your dharma is to teach others what you know, then by asking, 'How can I make this experience useful to my fellow human beings?' you may decide to share what you learned by writing a book about playing sports safely."[74]

Write a book? Gee, Deepak, you helped this fellow *human* being (ME!) by writing that last sentence. The doctor's illustration made my entire being whirl with joy and I tingled all over with the warm fuzzies. Now I *knew* that my intense emotional turmoil had merely been a way to push me along my life path, and suddenly...*shift happened*. Maybe I didn't have to carry the karmic burden of a gnarly Voodoo lifetime and suffer in the here and now? Writing a book about spiritual concepts might transmute my karma.

Abraham, *The Celestine Prophecy*, and Deepak Chopra all disseminate the same principles: When we are on our path, miracles happen. There is unstoppable joy in our heart. The Universe draws to us (through synchronicity) the perfect people and situations (or books) for our journey to unfold.

The following from Dr. Chopra's book nearly knocked me off of my bed. Under the seventh spiritual law of success, the Law of Dharma, he claims we have "taken manifestation in physical form to fulfill a purpose.... You have a talent that is unique in its expression, so unique that there's no one else alive on this planet that has that talent, or that expression of that talent. This means that there's one thing you can do, and one way of doing it, that is better than anyone else...."[75]

Chopra then relates three parts to the Law of Dharma. First, realize our true spiritual self. Second, discover our unique talents. Third, serve our fellow human beings. "How can I help? How can I assist all those with whom I come in contact?" When we combine the ability to express our unique talents with service to others, we are making full use of the Law of Dharma.

According to Chopra, "What's in it for me?" is the internal dialogue of the ego, or shadow self. Asking, "How can I help?" is the internal dialogue of our spirit. Our spirit is the domain of our awareness—where we experience universality with all.

His words lasered through the gray matter between my ears, and I recognized that the entire process of writing this book was a way to work through my own karma. A tremendous surge of joy and appreciation washed over me. I stretched out on my bed, tears streaming down my cheeks. TBIF had been the biggest gift in my life. Because of them, I had found something that gave my life purpose. I gave thanks to the band for still cranking out tunes after all these years, and not giving up despite everything they'd been through.

I also thanked TBIF's wives and families for putting up with their touring schedules. It's a huge sacrifice. I could only imagine what a difficult strain that must put on their personal lives.

I thanked the Law of Karma, because after TBIF's super stardom waned, they began playing smaller venues where I could see them up close, which had allowed me to become entrained with their energy, ultimately triggering my unconscious to **Wake the Bleep Up**!

Lastly, I thanked the fans for still attending TBIF's concerts, so we could all stand together…reflecting each other's souls. Now I could see that we are all one.

I'd read numerous self-help books about how to live a happier, more successful life, but my life's purpose could only materialize from following my own heart and intuition. Every day, my ego-shadow was still taunting me that pursuing a spiritual journey with the band was ludicrousness. Yet my heart and intuition encouraged me to continue despite my doubt. Amazingly, I did not choose my life path—my life path had chosen me.

As Deepak Chopra alludes, we all incarnate in physical form to fulfill a purpose. We each have talents so unique in expression that no one else on this planet has our particular gifts to share. Deepak was right. No one else on earth could possibly have written this book but Gawk Girl. It's my dharma.

CHAPTER 26

"SURRENDER"

—U2

"Much more than listening to beautiful sounds or music, spiritual attunement to the Sound Current within is the process for liberating soul from the clutches of mind, emotion, and illusion.... The Sound can heal the deep-seated karmic conditions that limit all seekers and keep us from experiencing the contact with the God within, which we so fervently desire."[76]   —Dennis Holtje, author

Deepak Chopra helped me shift into a new perspective. Now what would I do with it?

I set an intention for the Universe to bring me a dramatic clarity to my journey. I must be near the end! Would I be able to prove a group past life with TBIF and the fans after all? What about healing? Did I still need to heal something? Wasn't I finished with that stuff? *Patience, little Grasshopper. Patience.*

Vacations are healing—so off I went to California for TBIF's next tour: five concerts that spanned the length of the enormous state. It would be a road trip like none I'd ever experienced.

While driving my rental car from Los Angeles to San Diego to connect with other fanatics, I hooked up with my pen pal Sundante. She graciously introduced me to several other long-time fans, and everyone was nice as pie. Yet as we engaged in conversation, a little voice in my head bellyached, *You don't belong here. They don't really like you. They have a sense of humor. You are just so unfunny. Everything you say is awkward, out of place, and retarded. Just shut up and smile. Maybe they won't think you're such a dimwit.*

Whoa!!! Where was this coming from? This inner voice was really starting to piss me off.

At the concert that evening, TBIF started with an acoustic set and played a tune I hadn't heard *live* in about a zillion years. It was that bizarre "Colorado" song, the one about clues, south, east, and rivers. Was this a sign from the Universe to be on the *lookout* for something important?

A few minutes after the concert, I strolled to the end of my aisle to wait for Sundante, where I caught sight of the singer coming out of the stage area. An entourage encircled him, shuffling in sync around him. He stared straight ahead and sashayed right past me like I wasn't there, and an inner electrical current zapped me.

Two minutes later, the lead guitarist slowly walked past, with a white towel over his head. I'd seen him do this "ostrich head-in-the-sand, maybe-they-won't-see-me-and-ask-for-an-autograph" move at another concert. He came so close, I could have pulled off the towel. But I kept my hands to myself. He slinked past with their tour manager. The "Casper the Unfriendly Ghost" routine left me shell-shocked.

What's up Mr. Guitarist? You paid attention to me a few months ago at the Eugene and Boulder shows, and when I held up the sign in Denver. Ya don't remember the girl with the sparkly hat? Obviously not.

Sundante then joined me, and we headed over to where a group of fans were bantering and telling TBIF stories, having a grand ol' time. Gawk Girl felt ridiculously out of place. They were genuinely funny; I wanted to run and hide. Where were these *uncomfortable* feelings coming from?

The next morning, I joined several of the fans for breakfast.

As we ate, again painful feelings of separateness twisted inside me. These were very nice people. Why did I feel so awkward and *not* funny around them?

On my drive back to Los Angeles, these worries absorbed me. Why on earth did I feel so stupid around the other fans?

In a flash, I recalled sitting in a meeting with a bunch of radio sales reps at the station I had worked at eons ago. Those "type A" personalities were supremely witty, casually zinging out one-liners with great aplomb. No one ever noticed how quiet I was. When speaking individually with them, words easily emanated from my mouth; but when the room was full of their shiny personalities, my brain melted. I could not compete. I just sat in awe of their verbal shootouts. Research Girl became Invisible Girl.

Now, a decade later, I was feeling the same lack of self-esteem among the fans. Instead of joining in the fun, something inside me went "poof." No one was seeing me, not even the band.

Several days later, TBIF performed at a gigantic amphitheater outside of L.A., with other classic rockers such as Yes, Foreigner, and Journey. I saw Sundante right before TBIF came on stage. She was all excited because Tower Records had tables behind the amphitheater and if you purchased one of TBIF's CDs, the band would lovingly sign it. She had gotten their John Hancocks and asked if I knew about the signing.

No, *of course* I didn't. She'd met the band, like, a zillion times purely by accident in hotels, bars, or on escalators. *Her* psychic compass was set on "bump into band." My vibration was dialed on "let's play keep away."

When TBIF took the stage, it was still hot and sunny out, despite being the late afternoon. Dressed in sandals, shorts, and a cute orange sleeveless top, I actually wore my black sparkly hat. I looked ridiculous.

Our seats were in the far last row of the amphitheater, but a Jumbotron screen allowed us to see the performance quite nicely. Nevertheless, something nudged at me to get closer to the stage. It seemed important that the band know I was at the concert. *They need to see me* repeated incessantly in my cranium. So, I meandered down further to some empty seats.

I was still half-a-light-year away and couldn't get any closer. How could I get them to notice me? Think, think, think. Hey, my hat! If I stood up, the sun might bounce off my sparkles! They'd see my sparkly hat and know I was here!

In reality, unless I inflated to the size of Paul Bunyan, there was no way the band would see me, hat or no hat. I stood anyway, just in case one of them had a funky secret bionic telescopic eyeball that would catch my intermittent sparkly flashes.

What was I thinking this would accomplish? Send a secret Morse code to the band? I had no clue; I just felt compelled to get closer.

I didn't really want to meet TBIF. The thought still made me way anxious. But I knew I wanted them to see *me*.

After their set was over, I despondently returned to my original seat. Why did making contact matter so much? I wondered. Maybe because they're part of my soul group, my *brothers*? Each of us *is* a mirror to one another. Were the band and fans reflecting back to me my own lack of self worth? Right now, apparently my reflection was invisible.

During my drive to the next TBIF concert, a county fair in the booming metropolis of Bakersfield, my mind drifted back to a time when a stage hypnotist had come to my college. James Mapes' show was the first time I'd seen someone under hypnosis, and his work greatly influenced my interest in hypnotherapy and the subconscious. Several fellow students whom I personally knew wound up on stage—and talked to little green men under their chairs that only they could see. It was apparent to me that this was not just an act.

At the end of the routine, Mapes regressed three other students back in time to their childhoods, then to past lives. Their detailed descriptions of other lifetimes blew my mind...and sparked my initial curiosity in reincarnation.

At the Bakersfield concert, I'd had no idea which warm-up band would perform before TBIF. Imagine my surprise when a hypnotist walked on stage and asked for volunteers from the audience. Two-dozen high school students screamed, "Pick me!"

The dude's show was highly entertaining. People on stage answered their "phones" (actually their shoes), and jumped out of their seats in alarm every time the hypnotist touched his own forehead.

"Who pinched me?" they cried. No one had. We in the audience all laughed.

I had known intellectually that reality exists only within the *human* mind. To see such a literal example, again, however, blew me away.

I also had never witnessed a hypnotist perform before as a warm-up to a rock concert. Why the memory and synchronicity now? Was there a bigger *message* the Universe was trying to pound into my little cerebellum? Ahh. I get it. Our subconscious is the *hidden* part of our psyche.

Later that night, I looked through my bag of jewelry and found the necklace with the Nordic rune symbol, Perth, which means to bring something *hidden* to *light*. A sign of things to come?

Another important synchronicity had popped up during the Bakersfield performance. Several hours before the concert, Sundante was already in line. When I arrived, we asked some fans to hold our spot, and I dragged her out into the scorching heat to get a funnel cake. She'd never eaten one before! After consuming the greasy, sugar-powdered fried bread, we got back into line next to several long-time fans. One guy's personality was a cross between Robin Williams, Steve Martin, and Eddie Murphy. He blasted hilarious comments every thirty seconds, and his girl-friend gave him a run for his money in the ha-ha department. Oh no, jocular, slap-stick people all around me! *Help! I'm turning into Invisible Girl! I'm fading…I'm fading…*

To me, a fate worse than death is lobbing a clever pearl of uncontested wit into a crowd, only to have it land in a vast, black pit of silence. As the chasm yawns wider, everyone gets that *look* on their faces, the one where you can hear them thinking: Ewwww, I'm *sooo* embarrassed for her.

My old mental tapes started playing again. *You haven't got a funny bone in your body. You don't belong here.* Well, thank you, God. Thanks for creating the Law of Attraction. Love it.

But this time, instead of giving power to my old mental recordings, something inside of me just let go. Maybe it was the funnel cake, but *shift happened.* I *surrendered* in the moment and decided it would be okay to say something incredibly stupid, get it out of my system, and embrace the potential humiliation. So I did.

By the grace of a benevolent deity, my remark was actually kind of amusing. My offhand comment broke the damn, and then you couldn't shut me up. I joked and laughed and had a great time.

Being Humorless Girl was a self-fulfilling prophecy. The fans, like a mirror, had merely reflected back to me my own fears.

Changed my thoughts, changed my reality. If soul groups are drawn together to heal their past, mine was doing a rockin' job after all. Reality doesn't bite, it transforms!

After the concert, I caught up with yet another fan from Salt

Lake City whom I'd met at the Winter Park, Colorado show (serious TBIF fans really get around). She asked how my book was coming, and her husband, S, inquired what it was about. I told him it chronicles my journey to greater self-awareness through rock music, and he asked how I got such an unusual idea.

"I was told to write it," spontaneously burst out of my big mouth.

He pointed a finger to the sky. "You mean?"

"Yes!" I gushed.

S is a musician. He had worked as Frank Zappa's sound engineer for over a decade and had written several studio-recording engineering books…and he totally acknowledged my mystical inspiration to write about the healing power of music. I was thunderstruck.

I had been desperately wanting to connect with someone, *anyone*—even a monkey on roller skates would do—remotely interested in music *and* spirituality. Abracadabra, here he was. In five minutes, it felt as if we'd had a Vulcan mind-meld. We went to Denny's with a bunch of other fans for an hour or two and shared thoughts about the impact of music on our lives.

S related how he'd almost drowned as a teenager. Although a lifeguard had rescued him and he was fine, many years later, while viewing the original film version of *Titanic* on television, he had a sobbing meltdown. A torrent of memories flooded back regarding his near-death experience. He recalled hearing angels sing, bells, and other incredible sounds, which mystics attribute to the **Sacred Sound Current**.

I'd read about these sounds in several books. Our souls seem to have been created out of *sound,* yet the Sound Current isn't heard with our ears; it occurs at a subterranean level of consciousness into which few venture. Research indicates that a person typically needs to practice very deep meditation to *hear* the Sound Current. The Current is described in the book *Travelling the Sacred Sound Current* as the most beautiful sounds imaginable:

> As the soul ascends upon its journey along the Sound Current, a series of elemental sounds, each designating a specific spiritual region, become audible to the inner ear. Spiritual masters from different traditions have documented these with remarkable similarity. They include descriptions of an ascending ladder of sounds: the pounding surf of the sea, the humming of bees, the tinkling of soft bells, the running water of a brook, the chirping of birds, the rumbling of thunder, the roaring of a lion, the ringing of a loud bell, the blowing of a conch shell, the gong of a big drum, the strings of a harp, the tone of a flute, the sound of a bagpipe, the absence of all sound, and then the Great Soundless Sound which permeates all others.[77]

Sound can heal, transform, and connect us with our divine self. Dr. Michael Newton, author of *Journey of Souls* and *Destiny of Souls* (mentioned in chapter four), states that patients often hear sounds when regressed beyond their last death into the between-life state. One subject had described an echo, musical tingling, and wind chimes. Others had reported a relaxing sensation of musical vibrations. Newton says this music is appropriately called the *energy of the universe* because it revitalizes the soul.

Concerts certainly revitalize *my* soul and helped me transcend my Gawk Girl persona a bit. When the fans triggered my emotional wounding around humor, it provided an opportunity to move beyond my stuck patterns and be able to enjoy the witty, funny people I've always admired.

Years ago, I took a class on how to be a stand-up comic. I totally bombed. Not the right avenue for me. Now I was discovering that humor comes naturally when I write. With no audience to throw tomatoes, I can let it rip.

God has a wicked sense of humor. Write a book about group reincarnation *and* rock music? I mean, how much funnier can you get?

Rimshot. Ta da!

CHAPTER 27

"SEX AND THE CHURCH"

—David Bowie

"Rock concerts are the churches of today. Music puts them on a spiritual plane. All music is God"[78]

—Craig Chaquico, guitarist

Great rock songs have great guitar hooks. Musical hooks are as alluring to fans as chum is to sea bass. Wanna know what hooks me? When fans shine their side-splitting light beams all over the place. That hooks me big time.

I'm also hooked on wanting to know why spiritual talk seems to make most fans, aside from Sundante and S, run as though I'm Godzilla with bad breath. You know how I said people who hardly know me often share their spiritual and metaphysical stories? Well, among fans of TBIF, spiritual talk is mostly a dead zone.

Here's an example. Years ago, I took classes in hypnotherapy and, not long after, wound up standing next to a young guy at a TBIF concert who was becoming a hypnotherapist. Totally psyched, I blabbered on about regressing people to help them heal from their past-life issues. He looked at me as if a horn had just grown out of my forehead. He was only interested in weight loss and smoking cessation, and he thought I was nuts.

Back when I conducted my fan survey, I posted on TBIF's message boards asking if anyone thought the music deeply touched their souls. One person responded, yes; two made fun of the question. Not exactly stellar responses.

These kinds of reactions made me shy away from discussing reincarnation and spirituality with TBIF fans. Yet according to my rock-music survey, 30 percent of the general-rock fans indicated an interest in spirituality; but mention it to TBIF devotees, and most of them disappear like David Copperfield's white bunny rabbits. If I hadn't felt such a strong connection to the band, and regarded many of the fans as companion souls, their blank stares wouldn't have bothered me. But it way mattered.

So I wondered, why did I feel compelled to share my spiritual beliefs with the other fans? I didn't have a burning desire to proselytize to my friends who weren't interested in spirituality. My husband had no curiosity about the subject. So why my urgent push (for nearly a decade) to let TBIF fans know there is something important about the band's music … and that we need to **Wake the Bleep Up!** ?

Think, think, think. Excuse me. I'm having a Tao of Pooh moment.

Oh, thanks, Pooh.

How could I have been so blind? I care because, to me, music is a *spiritual medium*. Even though I'd read about the healing power of sound, my synapses had not before made the important connection: My spirituality gets activated around the other fans because the music triggers an almost *religious* feeling. It feels sacred. I'm more connected to my soul when the music is vibrating through my being. Jimi Hendrix was right on: "Rock music is more than music, it's like church!"

Hallelujah! I see the light!

On several occasions over the years, men have come up to me after concerts and commented on the intensity with which I sing the songs, how "into" the music Gawk Girl is. When TBIF's music hits my aural G-spot, I must look like Meg Ryan in the movie *When Harry Met Sally*. Not ecstatically screaming, "Oh,

Oh, Oh," but there is a similar connection. The connection is sex, music, and God.

Remember my little ditty on entrainment? When two similar bodies are in close proximity, they begin to resonate, or entrain. Getting physically closer to the band over the past several years, and receiving some attention from the guitarist, had generated a sense of power in me. I thought it was coming from within.

Now, I've figured it out. The guitarist's attention made me feel special, made me feel loved, adored. Made me feel there was a karmic-chi, soul-recognition thing going on between us.

I felt myself becoming attracted to him. He gave me what I wanted—acknowledgment that Gawk Girl mattered, even if only for a few minutes at a concert.

This spark, this feeling of *connection* led to a really uncomfortable question to ask myself. Did I want to have sex with him or the other guys in the band? (Not all at the same time, mind you.)

After a few minutes of letting my body *and* mind deal with this question, my next response to myself was a big fat honking, "No! Definitely not." The deeper attraction wasn't about sex. So, what was the sheer ecstasy I was feeling at the concerts?

Months before, on a lazy Sunday morning, the phrase "Father, Son, and the Holy Spirit" had waltzed into my cranium. Then a really outrageous idea tangoed its way in: *Hey, that's just like Sex, Drugs, and Rock 'n' Roll!* Was there an esoteric connection between these two rhythmic phrases? I set the words out side by side in the layout of a cross, and contemplated associations between "Father" and "Sex."

My first reaction was: *They don't connect at all. Stop trying to connect the dots. There aren't any dots to connect!*

Then the dots started to merge, like ants heading toward a yummy picnic.

What is sex, after all, but a *union* between two people? In spiritual studies, God is often referred to as All That Is, a total *union* of everything, just like the *Chemical Wedding* in alchemy.

A paragraph in the book *Jesus and the Lost Goddess* confirmed my theory that there *is* a connection between sex and God: "The Hebrew word for 'knowledge' is *daath*, which also means 'sexual union.' Gnosis [intuitive understanding of intellectual truths] truly is 'knowledge' in the Biblical sense! It is the coming together of the opposites to such intimacy that they become one. It is God and Goddess making love and so restoring the primal unity of the Mystery. It is the One being two becoming One."[79]

Is sex God's way of reminding us of our divine nature? The ecstatic feeling vibrates our body to a higher level, getting us closer to God. Father = Sex.

So what exactly was I feeling at the concerts?

Since everything is vibration, and music is a pure form of vibration, it wasn't a desire to have sex but to love *myself*, to awaken to my true identity. TBIF's music was helping me reach that higher level of vibration. I was so infused with the energy of the music that I couldn't help but scream the lyrics at the top of my lungs and throw my head back like a woman in climax. Being in the music was a union with the ultimate lover, the Divine. This might explain why so many women want to shag musicians. Rock stars = Sex.

In his book *Tramps Like Us*, Daniel Cavicchi states how some Bruce Springsteen fans feel that going to a concert is almost a religious experience. In fact, the author notes that becoming a fan is often associated with the same enthusiasm as someone who converts to a different religion.

Having read numerous books that describe vibration as the essence of God, and that music can help us heal, it was incredible to me that I hadn't grasped this important concept before. No wonder it drove me crazy that TBIF followers weren't resonating with me in a "spiritual" way, because concerts are where I access my faith. This is my church. And when I'm at church, I want to talk about God! Rock music = Sex = Church.

When I asked fans in the survey to describe emotions they had felt during concerts, joy and bliss won hands down. As in many religious pilgrimages, some fans have traveled significant distances to experience the music that brings them great joy and inspiration. In metaphysical circles, it is widely accepted that when we feel elation, God's essence is flowing through us. To fans, a rock concert is our personal Mecca. So, it makes sense that we'd go to great lengths to be in the presence of the musicians who bring forth the soul-stirring music. Music is the closest thing to pure vibration in the physical body.

The music can be a powerful addiction, but for some fans (like me) it goes beyond the music. It extends to the musicians. Daniel Cavicci wrote that people often make the rock stars "God," a devotion to those who perform the music. Well, duh. Music is an expression of God, so some fans transfer the power of the *music* onto the persons performing it. The musicians become the *source* of the connection to spirit. Rock star = God?

Have we taken the power of the *music* and erroneously placed it in the hands of its creators? Though they are quite sexy, and in my own twisted mind, one guy reminds me of the hot and powerful Norse god Thor, it makes sense to me now why the intuitives Jalynn and Danae said there is a hidden *message* coming through TBIF's music. Rock stars are not gods—they are *messengers* of the divine.

Thousands of years ago, the Greek god Hermes (Mercury in Roman mythology) was a *messenger* between the Gods and us *humans*. Who fulfills the messenger role today? Rock musicians!

Why? Because musicians are conduits, channeling inspirational and healing vibrations to the masses. Both God and musicians are in the business of VIBRATION. Rock star = Messenger.

In an earlier Tarot review, I noted how priests = magicians = musicians. Now I'm learning musicians are not only messengers, but shamans, too. Shamans (*witch doctors*) "at times fill the role of priest, magician, metaphysician, or healer."[80] Talk about multitasking. They communicate with the spirit world and act as translators between physical and non-material realms. But what's really interesting is that shamans use drums, rattles, and chanting (vibration) to shift into an altered state of consciousness when healing someone. Shamans truly are doctors of sound and music.

And what do ya know? "Sex, Drugs and Rock 'n' Roll" *does* mirror Father, Son, and the Holy Spirit, since many shamans use indigenous drugs—plant hallucinogens—to facilitate their altered states. Anthropologist Marlene Dobkin de Rios found that across various shamanic societies she had studied, the use of drugs was "usually a magico-religious sense, within a ceremonial context, to celebrate or to contact the realm of the supernatural, to heal an illness, to diagnose its cause, to divine the future, or to promote social solidarity among men and women."[81]

Look at those key words she uses! Magic, religious, heal, divine, social solidarity (union). Hot diggity dog. My Father-Son-Holy Spirit intuitive poke *was* significant, leading to greater insights about music and spirituality.

Until the twentieth century, music was sacred in many cultures around the world, and used for religious ceremonies and healing the body, mind, and soul. Why, oh why, is that no longer true? What the *bleep* happened?

Today, radio, television, and the record industry bring music to the masses, but they've also turned it into a *business*. In our modern society, music is whored, and only profitable acts are financially supported. Music no longer focuses on revering the Almighty God. Today, it's the Almighty Dollar.

Music is not meant to be restrained or treated with irreverence. It reflects the Divine in motion. It's how we *hear* God. Music helps us remember our spiritual identity. Embraced by music, we *know* we are an aspect of God. We feel it.

Where do we find God? Everywhere. Even a rock concert at a county fair can be sacred. If rock music is a tool for our personal growth, imagine the shift in consciousness that could occur at concerts. What if everyone set an intention for healing? Maybe this is one way we could transform from our ego-shadow perspective of separateness to an understanding of unity?

Sex, drugs, and rock 'n' roll—any of these may at any time bring us a sense of unity. Conversely, they all can become habit-forming. Although addiction is frequently detrimental to our well-being, what if getting imprinted by rock music as a teen was part of our soul's plan? Could rock music be a positive addiction that hooks us until we heal our trauma? If God *is* vibration, and music *is* a healing force, might our obsession with music be our soul attempting to help us **Wake the Bleep Up!?**

God = Vibration = Rock 'n' Roll = Healing = Waking up

CHAPTER 28
"I STAND UP"

"...everyone was using tiny brushes and doing watercolors, while Jimi Hendrix was painting galactic scenes in Cinemascope. We are working in a field of mystical resonance, sound, and vibration...that's what makes people cry, laugh, and feel their hair stand up."[82]
—Carlos Santana, musician

Despite these mystical insights about music, I still didn't see what I was supposed to **Wake the Bleep Up!** to about group reincarnation with TBIF and the fans. Why had my soul turned my life inside out? Why a wild-goose chase with synchronistic clues, leading to *where*?

Since healing trauma is a theme in group-reincarnation studies, and music is a healing force, the day I attended the final show of TBIF's tour, at a casino in Redding, California, I asked the Big Cheese to help me heal my funky fears.

God, stop wasting my time! I'm tired of feeling anxious around the band. If group reincarnation with TBIF is real, then show me what the bleep I need to heal.

Ask, and it is given.

But be careful what you ask for, Laura.

Tonight, Gawk Girl wanted to look all girlie. I wore a sparkly beaded sleeveless top with a high Chinese neck, perfect for a casino show. As a stay-at-home mom with two pre-school-aged girls, getting decked out happened like, *never*, so I looked forward to strutting in my bling-bling threads. Tonight, once again, I wanted to be seen. I wasn't sure exactly why I wanted to be a beacon, because a part of me was very apprehensive about looking so bright and shiny.

Since my one-notch-below circus-sideshow-freak height makes me stand out among most folks except the L.A. Lakers, walking into the casino dressed to the nines took enormous courage. On the inside, I was actually the cowardly lion's cousin, a scaredy-cat with a sparkly hat, afraid of other's opinions. "Who do you think you are? Show off! Giant mutant girl!" Blah, blah, blah.

Why did I give a flying rat's ass what anyone thought of me? I'd always been afraid of making mistakes, doing something that would piss people off. Miss Goody Two-Shoes wanted to be perfect so everyone would like her.

So, I took a deep breath. All right, Universe. Whatever you've got in store for me, bring it on.

Beneath my scintillating top, the Sanskrit necklace Sundante had given me for my birthday—fearlessness—promised courage. Could I muster it?

When I wondered if I'd accidentally collide with the band, my stomach did the funky, knotty, twisty dance. I'm growing weary of this ego-shadow nonsense.

Yet sometimes the only way to get over a fear is to go through it. Bloody hell.

While getting ready for the concert, I rang up Sundante, who excitedly gushed, "I saw the singer walking through the casino lobby and gave him a great big bear hug."

Of course she did! Sundante always played bumper cars with the band. She wasn't panic-stricken to meet them, so naturally the Law of Attraction drew them to her.

Me? I was still shakin' in my boots that they'd see me and

think "Goober Girl" if I simply said "Hello." Just call me Basket Case.

At the casino, I hooked up with Sundante and we hung out in the lobby before the show. My heart skipped a beat every time I caught a glimpse of a roadie or the tour manager. But no sign of the band. Whew. I was about to spontaneously combust. Where were those damn Rolaids?

After what felt like a year and an eternity, it was finally show time! The concert was in a huge ballroom. My second-row seat was on the middle aisle, directly in front of the singer, on the bassist's side of the stage. TBIF did not do an acoustic set list. Instead, they launched into their opening song. I immediately stood, as did a few other people. Then everyone sat down pronto. Huh? In previous casino shows, everyone had stood from the beginning to the last note.

Something, nevertheless, was pushing me upward. *Stand alone in my sparkly hat and shirt? Are you kidding?* I argued in my mind. *No flippin' way.*

So I sat. I looked over toward S and his wife. She was all the way out in the side aisle dancing. I was tempted to join her, and do my Buddy Ebsen hoofer imitation. But I squirmed in my seat like I had ants in my pants, and remained seated like every other lemming. Sit, sit, sit.

Was this a rock concert, or a geriatric ward? Why wasn't anyone standing? Why wouldn't these bench warmers do what I wanted them to do? How dare they sit, tonight of all nights! The band must see me!

It was the strangest feeling, this compulsion to stand, as though I'd already done it. Not in a déjà vu sense, more like following a script. Dr. Newton describes in *Destiny of Souls* how before we incarnate, our soul often sees important moments of our future life.

I felt as though the director (my spirit guide) had given me a specific role: Stand in your sparkly hat and shirt. In rehearsals, the other fans had stood, too. Maybe the script had been revised and no one told me?

If my soul did know the future (it told me I'd write a book and here it is), wouldn't it know what would unfold at this concert? I had planned my sparkly attire months ago, sensing this was a pivotal show. So why weren't things turning out the way they were supposed to? Was my soul group playing a trick on me?

The set was three-quarters over before a few fans finally stood during a well-known song—but on my side of the theater everyone remained seated. Total bummer! (Later, I would find out that the casino had a "no standing" policy. Sorry. Making fans stay seated during a rock concert is the most retarded thing I've ever heard of.)

Nevertheless, with everyone around me politely sitting, a voice in me yelled, *Stand now! Do it NOW!*

With a sudden burst of inspiration, the music gave me a jolt of courage and … *shift happened.* I stood.

I don't remember if I sang the lyrics. I don't know if the people behind me were pissed because they couldn't see past my big head. All I remember is feeling like a complete jackass. As tall as **Joey Ramone** (may Joey R.I.P.) in my heels, wearing the scintillating hat and shirt, I could double for the lighthouse at Montauk Point. I longed to be teeny tiny, to blend into the sea of fans.

The band didn't look at me…the only soul standing for several songs. "Please sit down! You're hurting our eyes." I imagined them thinking. But during the last few tunes, a bunch of female fans ran up the aisle toward the stage, despite the "no standing policy" and stood near me.

It's about time!

The last song is one of my favorites. I love the lyrics. It's about praising a woman. While crooning away, the singer points to various chicks in the audience at every concert. Tonight, as he singled out several women, he seemed slightly irritated. Then he pointed to a woman in a baseball cap with the band's name. She was standing right next to me. Two inches away. The singer smiled and mouthed to her, "I like your hat."

I couldn't believe it. I had wanted the band to see me, but tonight, I was Invisible Girl.

The concert ended, and I stood in shock for a few moments. Did my soul screw up, or what?

Then, swift as a cheetah, a two-by-four descended from the heavens and whacked me between the eyes. Wait a minute. I had asked the Universe to help me face my fears, and look what I got! An opportunity to confront my inner boogers and self-doubt. I received exactly what I asked for. Fans sat, while Sparkly Laura had taken a brave and bold stance! For once, I didn't follow the flock.

What an incredible metaphor to symbolize my journey and book. My bizarro view of rock music and spirituality sets me apart from other fans. I'm going against the mainstream. The masses sit, while I, with a different perspective, stand. Wow.

After I walked out of the ballroom, a lonely nickel-slot machine begged me to keep it company. Instead of ca-chinging my Thomas Jefferson's into it, however, I closed my eyes. The array of dinging bells and loud noises was mind boggling.

I picked one group of tones and zoned in. Out of the cacophony, the chaos, I found order. Then I heard something quite beautiful. The mind-numbing noise had created a kind of altered state, time suspended, and I entered the Sound Current.

Behind the bedlam, under the surface, everything was running smoothly. The script hadn't been revised. Everything unfolded exactly as planned. This gave me a sense of trust that all was well, and I could now let go of trying to control the events of my life. For the first time, it really sank in: I was being guided by my omnipotent soul.

CHAPTER 29

"A LIFE OF ILLUSION"

—Joe Walsh

"The essence of art...should reveal something that's hidden.... When that's working, it has power—power to heal and change."[83]   —Roseanne Cash, musician

Rapture soared though me! I wasn't just a separate, physical being. Something far more amazing than I had ever dreamed had given me the courage to walk the trail of self-actualization, and I wanted everyone to feel my supernova of joy!

Eventually, the feeling of bliss subsided. However, a residue lay in its wake—trust. Trusting that the Divine was directing my life during these California shows now provided a sense of relief for the road ahead. I could explore my fears and surrender my will to a higher power: my soul.

But as in TBIF's black-and-white checkerboard motif, life is a *cycle* of contrasts. We weave *between* the dark and the light, discovering who we are through the process. Though it seemed I had conquered my lack of self-worth, mucho layers of ego-shadow still needed to be peeled away. Cover your eyes. It isn't pretty.

Several days after my return home from the casino show, concert reviews from other fans rolled in on the band's message boards. One woman had run into the guitarist several times throughout the week, which made me glum. It seemed like everyone in the intergalactic cosmos had bumped into the guys except me. Apparently, it wasn't part of my script to meet them. Fine. But my boo-hoos were germinating deep down.

I kept replaying the moment when the singer had pointed to the woman next to me. It may have been my loco imagination but, real or not, I saw anger in his eyes during the song and for some reason, anger slowly burned within *me.*

Before heading out to the California concerts, I had scheduled an appointment with Carolyn (the Barbara Brennan energy worker). Good thing. I needed it. I didn't know how to deal with these continuing disturbing feelings. At the beginning of the session, I mentioned how the singer had singled out the chick with the band's baseball hat right beside me. Suddenly it hit me. Hey, what about *my* lovely hat?

"He points to ladies at *every* show," I said in a snit to Carolyn, "but never at *me!*"

"So you feel like he was mocking you?" she observed.

The words cut through me like a fishing knife. *Mocking me?*

She asked me to stand and feel the anger in my body. It was in my solar plexus, along with indignation and grief.

She then said to pull the energy down lower into my body, to really get in touch with my emotions. Well, I did, and an onslaught of rage torpedoed through me. I wailed and cried as if the singer was standing in front of me. "You don't get me! Here I am, terrified of being seen, and you mock me. I'm so bleeping pissed off. You don't know who I am! You don't have a bleeping clue! You stood there and judged me, you bleeping bastard! Bleep! Bleep! Bleep!"

Carolyn asked me questions about my childhood and, in a flash, my whole bleeping past came barreling in on me. Horrific memories of my seventh-grade repressed pain and humiliation suddenly came to mind. I bent toward the floor and a primal scream surged out of me. It was a massive release, worthy of an Academy Award for Scariest Pissed-Off Female. Totally blindsided me. Wow. A rock star was triggering Gawk Girl's buried anger from junior high? How freakin' twisted was I?

After the session with Carolyn, I met with my acupuncturist. He helped me to integrate more loving energy into my heart. As I lay on the table, my anger dissipated.

My journey down the Rock 'n' Roll Road sure was perplexing. Then I had an epiphany. Acupuncture treatments can do that sometimes. The person I had been most angry with was actually—me, not the singer or the kids he symbolized.

How many times had I agreed with someone because I was afraid to speak my mind, out of a fear of rejection? How many times had I pretended to feel one way but really felt another? More times than the number of stars in the galaxy.

I had been deceiving myself. Most of my life, my ego-shadow had convinced me to keep my mouth shut. *Don't express yourself and reveal the "real" you.* It was difficult to accept the truth. I was a pretender, a fake! Bloddy hell!

Two weeks later, I saw Carolyn again. Something still felt extremely out of whack. At this point, my mystical journey felt like *Mission Impossible.* I didn't believe I would ever muster the courage to publish this book. The idea of people thinking I was a flaky fraud for believing in past lives with a rock band, paralyzed me. Fans wouldn't like it. They'd be mad and throw tomatoes at my face.

I also told Carolyn how the guitarist had given me some attention, and I was confused about the mixed-bag of emotions he triggered. Carolyn said, "Do you want to be acknowledged for who you really are? Let's try something. Pretend you see the band in the hotel, walking past you. What do you say?" I made a flip comment and she replied, "That wasn't from the heart. Do it again. See me as the guitarist. Look me in the eye, and tell me what you want to say to me."

I took a deep breath and looked her in the eyes and … *shift happened.* What was hidden suddenly came to light. Frozen with astonishment, I slowly said, "All ... I ... can ... say ... is ... *repulsion.* Oh, my God. They are repulsed by me."

"Where does that come from?" Carolyn asked.

I hesitated. "I don't know. Another life? Holy shit, when I was a teenager...." I paused. "The bullies in school detested me. I was totally Gross Girl. Oh my God, I'm repulsed by *myself.*"

After a few moments, I made another association. "No, it can't be possible. I've turned the guys in the band into my tormenting seventh-grade bullies?"

I dug deeper. Over time, a bigger picture emerged. My bizarre fears and lack of self-worth stemmed not only from childhood, but unhealed past-life trauma. The school kids had found me totally gross, because the groups and ethnic backgrounds to which I had possibly belonged—Rosicrucians, Black soldiers, American Indians, Holocaust Jews—were outsiders. Their ideologies, skin color, and religion were frequently repulsive to others, so they were repressed or exterminated.

We can't overcome trauma from past incarnations unless a similar "vibration" gets triggered in this lifetime. So, my brilliant soul had chosen a perfectly tall body to help me feel unworthy around a perfect group of twelve-year-olds. Some kids had taunted, mocked, and teased me. Cool boys ignored me. Invisible Girl.

How can we know we're beautiful, worthy, or courageous, unless we're put into situations where we feel ugly, worthless, and fearful? It is in overcoming feeling repulsive or afraid that we get to know our self-worth. Through the Law of Attraction, I had been drawn to the perfect groups for me to heal my feelings of ickiness. As a kid, it was my seventh-grade classmates. Today, it was TBIF and the fans. So, of course, I had felt uncomfortable, an outsider, around the fans. When they laughed and joked with one another, my ego-shadow had freaked-out. They were laughing at *me.*

Even the light-hearted, wise-cracking lead guitarist was laughing at me in my mind. No wonder I was afraid to get too close to the stage all these years. I was terrified he'd discover me for who I really was. Super Gawk Girl. He'd really poke fun of me then. In reality, he wasn't, of course. He was merely connecting with me through his sense of humor. But my ego-shadow had no sense of humor. My ego's pain body was stuck in the past, so naturally I was skittish near him. Yet more than anything, I wanted his approval, to be a part of the gang, the brotherhood.

And the singer? Oh, my heavens. Cool, good-looking. The type of guy who had never given me a moment's notice in school. Non-entity me. No wonder I felt INVISIBLE around him and thought he avoided looking my way during concerts. Miss Lack of Self-Esteem unconsciously transferred her past trauma onto him. I guess that's what our unconscious ego-shadow does, transfers our inner-boogers onto others, to protect us from being hurt.

Oh, the irony! Our ego-shadow hides. It's *invisible*. We only see it when another person or situation triggers what we've repressed. Everything I had come to learn about soul groups (they act as our mirror so we can heal our trauma) I had played out with TBIF and the fans. How could this be possible?

A book on comparative myths yelled, "Hey, look at me! The answer is in here!" Lo and behold, the book opened to a page on the ancient Greek myth of Narcissus and Echo. In case you've forgotten, Echo had the hots for the vain, handsome dude, but she could only repeat what was said to her. When Echo saw Narcissus in the forest, she hid. He called out, but she sounded kinda stupid because she kept repeating his words. When Echo finally revealed herself, Narcissus took one look at her and said she was *repulsive*. She was so humiliated that she hid in a cave and wasted away. All that remained of Echo was the repeating wails of her voice in caves across the world.

Pass the Kleenex, please.

This ancient story smacked me upside the head. Reminded me of who? Duh. Myself. My old self, that is. I had been living the myth of Echo.

The word *echo* stems from the Greek *ekhe*, meaning "sound." That's curious, seeing as the whole theme of this book is about the healing vibration of sound. As mentioned earlier, resonance means "echo." An echo is a *sonic mirror*. The band was mirroring back to me my unconscious feelings of being repulsive. An echo repeats. We repeat lifetimes until we heal, the basis of reincarnation.

The late American mythologist, Joseph Campbell, lamented that in modern society we have lost our connection to myth and, therefore, our true selves. Myths provide a model, or blueprint, which *hu*mans unconsciously follow (like movie scripts). Mythic images are incredibly powerful because they have been validated by centuries of human history. They give us ideas for how to handle situations that arise in life. As with archetypes, myths are the very essence of our human culture, and show us how to be a fully integrated *hu*-man being. Nice to know that *now*.

Echo and I may seem to be twins in numerous ways, but my pity-party ended after thirty years—because *shift happened*. Amazingly, I entrained with the singer's anger (real or not, that's the vibe I picked up). His pointing was an unconscious signal in my mind to "get the point" that it was time to **Wake the Bleep Up!** to my own repressed rage. Like a magician, the singer's intention was encoded in the vibration of his singing voice. His voice (sound) acted as a carrier wave of consciousness.

Ah ha! That must be part of the hidden message in the music! I figured it out. Entrain with your favorite rock band, dredge up the buried inner boogers that have kept you stuck in the past, and transform your painful emotional baggage. This is one path to inner liberation and freedom.

When Echo revealed herself to Narcissus, she stood alone. Though standing alone was terrifying for me as well, my vibration *shifted* because the music at TBIF's concerts gave me the courage to face my unconscious boogeyman (my ego-shadow) and stand up to my fear of being rejected. Music was the key.

Earlier, Danae the intuitive had said that music creates a standing wave. Now I think I understand why in my Idaho dream the song "Helter Skelter" was sped up: When I was a kid, I used to run around in large circles in my basement, with my 33 rpm albums playing at 45 rpms. Weird, I know. I imagined standing up to the mean kids at school. The faster music made me feel invincible. By running in circles, perhaps I was inadvertently creating a standing wave, an energetic wall of protection?

Like Thor and Archangel Michael, rock musicians are mythological characters who provide protection. Musicians are truly armies of light. In many cultures, musicians have been essential members of the army. The beating and rhythm of a drum fosters a sense of protection for young warriors who face a terrifying enemy.

TBIF's music gave me the courage to be a warrior, and to reenact past situations that had generated fear. That's how rock music protects us. It helps us to feel powerful and heroic and face our greatest unseen enemy, the ego-shadow.

Since TBIF and their fans are part of my soul group, I had felt safe enough to act out my script—my myth—because I instinctively *knew* we are all warriors of light fighting to heal so we can be free of our emotional pain.

Long live rock 'n' roll!

CHAPTER 30

"I WALK AWAY"

—Crowded House

*"The music that really turns me on is either running toward
God or away from God. Both recognize the pivot; that God is
at the center of the jaunt."*[84]

—Bono, musician and philanthropist

After the post-concert therapy sessions, my focus shifted
from uncovering a past life with TBIF to the final phase of my
journey. I said bye-bye to reincarnation scenarios. *Done with you!*
But sometimes the things we've been asking for show up when we
least expect them.

Pertinent "messages" have often shown up for me while
sitting in waiting rooms, perusing magazines. Leaf through a
periodical and, abracadabra, an important insight appears.

While waiting for my chiropractor, I flipped through a
recent issue of the holistic journal *Nexus*. In a big, bold
font, the words "Return of the Revolutionaries: Evidence of
Reincarnation" dominated the back cover. Pictures of sixteen
well-known people from today were placed alongside portraits of
similar-looking persons from hundreds of years ago.

The ad copy read: "In his book, *Return of the
Revolutionaries: The Case for Reincarnation and Soul Groups
Reincarnated*, Walter Semkiw, MD has compiled compelling,
independently researched, reincarnation cases, which demonstrate that facial features, personality traits, and writing style stay
the same across lifetimes, and that people incarnate into karmic

groups. He also identifies leaders of the American Revolution who are reincarnated today."[85]

My jaw hit the floor. *You've got to be bleeping kidding me!* I had been begging the Universe to bring me people who resonated with my group-reincarnation idea, and here was a dude who had written an entire book on it. Love that Law of Attraction.

Dr. Semkiw's case study validated many concepts I had come to understand, such as: "A common feature in past-life research is that symbols from a prior lifetime are found in a person's contemporary incarnation."[86]

Symbol? Did someone say symbol? Like a band's black-and-white checkerboard motif? I grinned. This was getting *veeeery* interesting.

"Symbols and synchronistic events can provide clues as to who we were in past lives," wrote Semkiw. "They can also be seen as road markers along the paths of our predetermined destinies."[87] The black-and-white checkerboard was a marker, a clue—to the band and fans' past lives. Predetermined destinies indicate that we're following a script, or myth. Maybe Gawk Girl's psychic antennae were accurate all along!

Facial features, says Semkiw, are fairly consistent lifetime to lifetime. That's why the photo/portrait comparisons of a reincarnated soul often look like twins. I shivered with realization. When I had found Dr. Robert Fludd's portrait on a website, I had stared into his eyes with an immediate resonance, a soul recognition. To me, he looks just like one of the guys in the band. Stranger yet, Fludd was into face reading.

In the art of face reading (**physiognomy**) every feature of the face, teeth, and ears reflects our personality. Like the lined encoded messages on our palms, our face offers clues to our true identity. The intuitive Danae had told me, "The body's form in every incarnation is based on consciousness, so you manifest your physical body to express lifetimes you've lived. Your cellular memory…is not only what causes your physical features in this lifetime; it is also the experience of the living of emotions, of mental memories, and physical experiences."

Even the late **Dr. Ian Stevenson**, renowned psychiatrist and past-life researcher from the University of Virginia, found a high correlation between people who recall dying of a traumatic wound in a past life and birthmarks in the same location on their body in this lifetime. If Dr. Semkiw's observations are correct— that physical features remain fairly consistent over lifetimes—and if Dr. Stevenson's findings that a physical trauma may carry over onto our present body as a birthmark or scar, then our facial features and unusual physical markings may reflect our experiences from other lifetimes.

Take Oprah Winfrey, for instance. According to Dr. Semkiw, she was a white male abolitionist named James Wilson during the American Revolution. Semkiw wrote that their physical characteristics are similar despite changes in gender and race, and some personality traits carried over as well.

If our society were to grasp the concept of reincarnation, would war and discrimination eventually be eradicated? If we *knew* that all humans are literally one, and that we experience that oneness in different colored bodies and religious preferences, would we begin to realize the *brotherhood* of humanity?

In the book mentioned earlier, *Beyond the Ashes: Cases of Reincarnation from the Holocaust* by Rabbi Gershom, many memories of being persecuted during WWII are from gentiles, not Jews. This illustrates how karmically we may choose various ethnic and religious backgrounds to acquire a variety of earthly experiences. Each lifetime is literally a yummy smorgasbord! Our souls understand oneness. Now if we could just get our ego-shadows to stop being back-seat drivers, the future would be so bright we'd have to wear shades!

While reading Dr. Semkiw's writings, I became eager to discuss group reincarnation with him. Ask, and it is given. Not long after I returned home from the chiropractor, I was looking at **Carol Bowman**'s website on children's past lives. A posting I saw almost sent me into anaphylactic shock. Dr. Semkiw would be giving a talk in Boulder in a few weeks...and only ten miles from my house. A high-five from the Universe. Visualization + Vocalization = Manifestation. The Law of Attraction at work.

At his thought-provoking lecture, Dr. Semkiw shared his long journey to accepting that he had lived during the American Revolution. He recounted the incredible synchronicities that had occurred on his path, the clues he had followed. It all sounded *very* familiar. We met briefly after his talk, and I imparted my rock 'n' roll, past-life adventure. He encouraged me to share my reincarnation insights with others and to pursue publishing this book.

I should have been elated after our rendezvous, since I had finally met another group reincarnation enthusiast. Instead, my heart sank. Why? I wondered.

I realized it came back to the fear of publishing this book. Writing it was one thing. But making my journey public? Oh, God. Here came those damn twisty knotty stomach pains again. Dr. Semkiw didn't seem to have any gastro-intestinal upset about putting *his* group-reincarnation book out into the world. He wasn't afraid of getting rotten tomatoes thrown at him by an angry rock band and their fans.

Everything I had learned—to trust my soul's guidance and to believe in myself—went poof. Gone. I was regressing big time. A downward spiral of panic ensued. In this lifetime, the guilt of breaking the oath, of not keeping things secret, was ripping apart my psyche. I desperately wanted *shift* to happen, but the Universe *couldn't* give me a smiley face. Shift only happens when we are a *vibrational match* to what we want. We can't feel happy-happy joy-joy if our signal is stuck on "woe is me."

If your radio dial is set on 98.7 FM but you don't like the music, do you scream at the radio for playing classical when you want classic rock? Throwing a hissy-fit doesn't change the station. We have to change the dial. When we change our perspective (vibration), we open our mind—which means that *then* anything *is* possible.

As mentioned earlier, one definition of insanity is doing or thinking the same thing over and over, expecting a different outcome. I was repeatedly playing the same station—TBIF's music—hoping it would shift my vibration and create a force field (standing wave) to protect me. I prayed that these incessant fearful thoughts, coupled with the music, would free me from my guilt and flying tomatoes. This was a highly warped plan.

Instead, like a junkie who's built up a tolerance and needs more and more to get high, I had become obsessed with TBIF's music. *Gimme more intoxicating bass riffs, more pounding drums, more of the singer's soothing voice!* Shift did *not* happen.

For months, I was like a scratched record, stuck in my own repetitive groove of TBIF's music. Totally distraught, I realized there was no easy way out. If this lifetime was an opportunity to overcome my old fears, traumas, and addictions, then I damn well better find a way to shift my ego-shadow's obsession with the past and fear of the future.

The question was, how? I asked JC and the Tarot cards. The answer? The 8 of Cups. A person walks away from that which no longer serves, leaving the past behind and moving on.

NOOOOOO! Not that! I had to walk away?...From the band? Bloody hell!

"That's not fair!" I shouted to my walls covered with TBIF's posters.

Could I? Could I leave my *soul group* behind and move on with my life? What would it feel like to cut the cord?

At first, I couldn't even imagine such a thing. But welling up within me from the depths of my soul was the truth. My obsession with the band and their music was consuming my energy and blocking me from acknowledging my deeper fears.

To regain inner balance, I knew that I must stop depending on the band and their music to make me happy and secure.

It's time to stand on your own, my soul encouraged.

Was quitting cold-turkey realistic? I had devoted myself to their music for decades. Who was I beyond my attachment to the band? My identity was wrapped up in being a fan. Could I survive without TBIF or their music? I worried. I nodded to myself. I could. I had to.

Time to face the music. Time to say goodbye. TBIF's music no longer was serving my growth. It had become a crutch and an addiction.

To let go of TBIF, I decided to perform a ritual. It took me a few days to sort it all out and summon the strength. Then I gathered things that held meaning for me: a small stone obelisk with a black-and-white checkered pattern, a little wizard statue holding a crystal ball, a fossil (symbolizing eternity), my Tarot cards, and TBIF's first and latest CDs. I set these all around me and, with tears streaming, called upon JC and my highest guidance.

Then I reflected on how each fellow in the band symbolized a part of myself. The drummer's rhythms evoked a primal memory, the call of the warrior. He had entrained my heart with his drumming, coaxing my darker emotions to the surface where they would ultimately transform.

The bassist's intoxicating riffs had seized my entire being like a skilled hypnotist. His bass playing had flirtatiously invited me to come and have a good time. He is such a free spirit. When he smiles at a fan in the audience, his eyes light up and a sense of playfulness exudes from him. He reminds me of myself as a young child, when I delighted in being creative and having fun just for the sake of having fun.

The singer embodies raw power, not flashy or dramatic, very subtle. He seems calm on the surface, like an ocean undertow, but when he sings—watch out. He belts out every word with great *intent*, the magician's secret ingredient for manifestation and transformation. The singer reminds me of the part of myself who, like a magician, wants to help people transform from being ordinary into being *extraordinary*. He reflects my desire not to be afraid of my power, but to embrace it and use it with integrity for the highest good.

The guitarist is the "class clown," a joker, a trickster. He is a clever wordsmith, a lover of double entendre, and has symbolized the part of me who also wants to be humorous and spontaneous. That's his outward guise. On the inside, I sense that a river runs deep in his heart. Like me, he hides his emotions behind his persona, a mask.

Each man has represented a different archetype within me: the Warrior, the Child, the Magician, and the **Trickster**. But the Trickster, my favorite, isn't all about fun and games. He challenges and pokes fun at society's outmoded ways of thinking. Wow. It never occurred to me before that *I* am a Trickster, too; seeking to expose our big fat cultural lies about spirituality and reincarnation. Thanks, TBIF.

So I imagined the four band members as their archetypes, standing in the four corners of a square with me in the middle. I asked their souls to return the parts of myself I had given away to them over the lifetimes. Whatever energy of theirs I had, I requested it to be released from me and returned to their souls. I thanked each of them for being a catalyst for my journey and, on a bright sunny day in the year 2004, I stopped listening to their music. Gawk Girl, like the butterfly, finally metamorphosed into a *hu*-(wo)man. I spread my wings, threw away my crutch, and embraced the unknown.

The intuitive Heidi had said that people continue to listen to a band's music until they have absorbed the vibration into themselves. If that occurs, they may no longer feel a *need* to listen. I no longer *needed* TBIF's music to make me feel whole. I had discovered that all of the missing parts of myself—courage, power, humor, and playfulness—were always within me. They simply had been hiding in the shadows of my fear.

There comes a time when we all need to walk away and move on, even with music that has nourished us for a lifetime. Knowing when to let go is simply a part of the Fool's journey. It's a key to self-discovery.

By walking away, a door opened into a part of me that I hadn't known existed. When the doors of perception are cleansed, we see things as they really are. Infinite.

I Found All the Parts

PART FOUR

EPILOGUE

"IT'S THE END OF THE WORLD AS WE KNOW IT (AND I FEEL FINE)"

—R.E.M.

"The new composers will not only be virtuosos; they will be genuine mystics. Their mission will surpass the role of public entertainers and they will recover the great initiatory work of the creators of sacred music."[88]

—Patrick Bernard (Bernhardt), sacred chant musician

It's hard to believe that the bambina I rocked in my arms the night of my future memory vision is now seven years old. My two daughters were helping to put away clothes in my walk-in closet when they discovered my black sparkly hat hanging amidst a bunch of belts and scarves. It hadn't adorned my head in over four years, since the night of the Redding concert.

"Mom," my nine-year-old exclaimed, "this is sooo pretty! Why don't you ever wear it?"

"Why don't *you* wear it?" I beamed, tickling her ribs and reveling in her giggles. "I hear the Village People are looking for new singers."

She had no idea who I was talking about, and ran to the bathroom to put the hat on. It came down to her eyes, though underneath a smile broadened across her face as she admired herself in the mirror. Both girls giggled. They have no issues embracing their feminine beauty.

"Let me try," said my youngest.

They passed the black sparkly hat back and forth, then

finally pleaded with *me* to wear it. So, I bent over and they shoved it onto my head and we all burst out laughing. The sparkly hat was absurd with my old T-shirt and baggy jeans.

"When you're older, you can have it," I said to my daughters.

In unison they both cried, "Hooray!" and pranced out of the room, off to act out some imaginary story involving a wounded unicorn, some ponies, and a benevolent fairy.

I looked at the hat. Past lives with a rock band? My incredible journey still seemed like a twisted fantasy at times, though I knew it was very real.

I naively believed that my odyssey with TBIF was complete. No more repressed anger, buried emotions, or complexes lingering in my psyche. All those nasty inner-boogers healed. I would live happily ever after.

Got that wrong!

Much to my dismay, self-discovery is an ongoing, lifelong process, and doesn't end just because we finish what we started (like writing the rough draft of a book). To my surprise, my journey really kicked into high gear *after* I stopped listening to TBIF's music. Lots of shift happened.

All of the emotional tsunamis with TBIF were merely a preparation for an upcoming massive psychological earthquake—that hit me with a force that felt greater than the big bang. Without delving into all of the gory details (that's another story) let me just say that descending into the heart of darkness is a part of every Fool's journey...and it sucks. My ego-shadow has more guises and personalities than **Sybil**. Bloody hell.

The mega inner-goobers took a toll on my body and mind. But my spiritual growth with rock music had taught me to trust my soul's guidance. Sometimes, getting emotionally all shook up provides the necessary swift kick in the pants to wake us up, to deal with our unhealed past. No wonder we live numerous lifetimes. Our soul can't possibly handle all of our karmic crap during just one gig on earth. It would be too overwhelming for us.

For over a year, I shied away from anything having to do with TBIF. I explored alternative sound-healing therapies, mantras, **mudras**, and other holistic paths that ultimately brought me greater balance. As my psyche and body slowly healed, an inner voice nudged that my karma with TBIF was not complete.

I had remained friends with Sundante and, when I was ready to return, she kept me notified of band happenings. Although my sparkly hat didn't attend any more TBIF concerts, *I* did.

I stood in the audience no longer obsessed with four guys playing three great chords. Having plunged the depths of my soul, my perspective had changed. *I* had changed. It was incredible how far I had journeyed.

In 1997, during my first intuitive TBIF reading, Jalynn had said, "It feels to me that it is an energetic gathering of souls in preparation for something that is coming up.... Their music is a way of uniting the warriors of their old clan."

Now I *know* that rock music has a much bigger purpose. It goes far beyond fans and bands gathering for entertainment. Jake and Elwood Blues, The Blues *Brothers*, said it best: "We're on a mission from God."

Where exactly the Rock 'n' Roll Yellow Brick Road leads, I don't know. Will rock bands and their fans fulfill their karma and complete their spiritual mission from God? Well, if we **Wake the Bleep Up!** we will!

I can *guarantee* it will be one hell of a ride on the Marrakesh Express if we collectively embrace our woo-woo mystical side.

Despite great temptation, I kept my promise. I still haven't played any TBIF CDs. Well, kinda sorta. There was a new release in 2006—but that's the only one. My intuition nudged me—poke, poke, poke—that there were tunes I needed to hear on that CD. Turns out, the song lyrics acted as a humongous backhoe in my psyche, and unearthed *more* unconscious inner-boogers than I cared to know about. Like the Energizer bunny, insights and healings keep coming, and coming, and coming.

But, at long last, the compulsive need to listen to TBIF's enduring and intoxicating music no longer consumes me. I've found my inner balance, at least for now. Fingers crossed, knock on wood, with a four-leaf clover in one hand, and a rabbit's foot in the other.

Superstitions aside, there is no such thing as good or bad luck. It's all a matter of paying attention to our intuition. Synchronicity is a high-five that the Universe is talkin' to us, and is beautifully described by the author of *Future Memory*, P.M.H. Atwater. Several years ago, I emailed Atwater about my mystical journey. This is her remarkable response:

> When we ask sincerely, the universe responds. We are heard, and because we are, a string of "now" moments begin to arrange themselves as connecting links in a new streamer of consciousness awaiting our energetic involvement. We call these "now" moments "synchronicity," for lack of a better term. They're part of how life's web operates; new streamers extend and interweave the fabric of consciousness and enlarge what can be experienced. What triggers the "now" moments? Visions. Near-Death Experiences. Vision Quests. Prayer. Meditation. Baptism of the Holy Spirit. Spiritual Transformation. Maybe an accident that significantly challenges us and what we think we believe. Maybe the simple but heart-felt desire to be a better person does it.

Whatever is our trigger, the result is always a change in our consciousness—a transformation of sorts that can be partially or deeply involved or a radical shift in perception—followed by cascades of insight, future-memory episodes, rushes of bliss and joy, increased energy, heightened intuition and creativity, an urge to learn more and do more and be more, changes in our body-mind structure/functioning.

How do we label such an event? We don't. It is the aftereffects that assign purpose and meaning. Did Laura have a near-death-like experience? A future-memory episode? A peak experience of spiritual enlightenment? I cannot say, for there are elements of what happened to her in all these types of sudden shifts in consciousness. What matters to me is what she did about her episode, and where it led her. Therein lies the good news of Laura Faeth.

Not one sheet of Kleenex remained in my house after reading Ms. Atwater's email. What a powerful message.

The Celestine Prophecy says that everyone we meet has a message for us. Rock musicians, guys with binoculars at a concert, authors. Everyone is a messenger. We are *all* here to remind each other—poke, poke, poke—of our true spiritual identity.

Visionary musician Torkom Saraydarian is definitely a messenger. He wrote, "Music in the coming centuries will play a greater role than the roles played by physics, chemistry, and engineering combined. Through the utilization of sound, many scientific discoveries will be rendered obsolete. It will be possible through music to lead nations and humanity to a higher realization of divine principles."[90]

There is no doubt that the brotherhood of rock music has changed the landscape of our lives and influenced cultures socially, politically, even spiritually. The music certainly caused a revolution in my world.

Sound and music are fundamental tools of our *hu*-man existence and always have been. Whenever we hear the beating of a drum, we get a twinkle in our eye and our body starts moving in absolute joy. We can't help but do the cosmic cha-cha-cha. No matter what the future holds, like the immortality of our spirits, the echoes of rock 'n' roll will never fade.

ROCK ON!...AND ON!...AND ON!

BIBLIOGRAPHY AND RECOMMENDED READING

Andrews, Ted. *Sacred Sounds, Magic & Healing Through Words & Music,* St. Paul, MN: Llewellyn Publications, 1992.

———. *Dream Alchemy: Shaping Our Dreams To Transform Our Lives,* St. Paul, MN: Llewellyn Publications, 1991.

Atwater, P.M.H. *Future Memory,* Charlottesville, VA: Hampton Roads, 1999.

Bengston, David. *Past Lives of Famous People: Journeys of the Soul,* Woodside, CA: Bluestar Communications, 1997.

Berent, Joachim Ernst. *The World is Sound: Nada Brahma,* Rochester, VT: Destiny Books, 1983.

Berg, Yehuda. *The 72 Names of God: Technology for the Soul,* Los Angeles, CA: Kabbalah Publishing, 2003.

Boyd, Jenny, Ph.D. *Musicians in Tune,* New York, NY: Fireside, 1992.

Braden, Greg. *The God Code,* Carlsbad, CA: Hay House Inc., 2004.

Browne, Sylvia. *A Psychic's Tour of the Afterlife, Life on the Other Side,* New York, NY: Dutton Adult, 2000.

Bunning, Joan. *Learn the Tarot: A Tarot Book for Beginners,* York Beach, ME: Red Wheel/Weiser, 1998.

Byrum, Larry. Higher Alignment and The Institute for Spiritual Partnership, class handout.

Campbell, Joseph, with Bill Moyers. *The Power of Myth,* New York: NY: Anchor Books, 1991.

Cavicchi, Daniel. *Tramps Like Us,* Oxford, England: Oxford University Press, 1998.

Chamberlain, Richard. *Shattered Love,* New York, NY: Harper Collins, 2003.

Chopra, Deepak. *The Seven Spiritual Laws of Success,* San Rafael, CA: Amber-Allen & New World Library, 1994.

———. *The Spontaneous Fulfillment of Desire: Harnessing the Infinite Power of Coincidence,* New York, NY: Harmony Books, 2003.

Craven, J.B. *Dr. Robert Fludd: The English Rosicrucian,* Whitefish, MT: Kessinger Publishing; Facsimiled edition, 1992.

Cunningham, Janet. *A Tribe Returned,* Crest Park, CA: Deep Forest Press, 1994.

Emoto, Masaru. *The Hidden Messages in Water,* Hillsboro, OR: Beyond Words Publishing, 2004.

Fast, Susan. *In the Houses of the Holy, Led Zeppelin and the Power of Rock Music,* Oxford, England: Oxford University Press, 2001.

Freke, Timothy and Peter Gandy. *Jesus and the Lost Goddess,* New York, NY: Crown Publishing, 2002.

Friedman, Norman. *Bridging Science and Spirit,* Eugene, OR: The Woodbridge Group, 1990, 1997.

Gershom, Yonassan. *Beyond the Ashes: Cases of Reincarnation from the Holocaust*, Virginia Beach, VA: A.R.E. Press (Association of Research & Enlightenment), 1992.

Godwin, Joscelyn. *Harmonies of Heaven and Earth*, Rochester, VT: Inner Traditions International, 1987.

————. *Robert Fludd*, Grand Rapids, MI: Phanes Press, 1991.

Goldman, Jonathan. *Healing Sounds* (2nd Edition), Rochester, VT: Healing Arts Press, a division of Inner Traditions, 1992, 2002.

————. *The Lost Chord-liner notes*, Etherean Music, 2000.

Guirdham, Arthur. *We Are One Another*, Essex, England: C.W. Daniel Co. Ltd., 1974, 1991.

Hart, Mickey. *Spirit into Sound: The Magic of Music*, Petaluma, CA: Grateful Dead Productions and Acid Test Productions, 1999.

Hart, Mickey and Jay Stevens. *Drumming at the Edge of Magic: A Journey into the Spirit of Percussion*, Petaluma, CA: Grateful Dead Productions and Acid Test Productions, 1998.

Hayes, Mike and Ken Sharp. *Reputation is a Fragile Thing*, Willow Grove, PA: Poptastic!, 1998.

Head, Joseph and S.L. Cranston. *Reincarnation: The Phoenix Fire Mystery*, New York, NY: Julian Press Inc., 1977.

Hicks, Esther. *Abraham-Hicks Daily Planning Calendar and Study Group Workbook*, San Antonio, TX: Abraham-Hicks Publications, 1996.

Hodapp, Christopher. *Freemasons for Dummies*, Hoboken, NJ: Wiley Publishing, 2005.

Javane, Faith and Dusty Bunker. *Numerology and the Divine Triangle*, Atglen, PA: Whitford Press, 1979.

Jenny, Hans. *Cymatics*, Newmarket, NH: MACROmedia, 2001.

Jung, Carl. *Jung on Active Imagination*, Princeton, NJ: Princeton University Press, 1997.

Khan, Hazrat Inayat. *The Mysticism of Sound and Music*, Boston, MA: Shambhala Publications, Inc., 1991.

Marciniak, Barbara. *Bringers of the Dawn*, Rochester VT: Bear & Co, a division of Inner Traditions, 1992.

Montano, Mary. *Loving Mozart*, Albuquerque, NM: Cantus Verus Books, 1995.

Myss, Caroline, Ph.D. *Why People Don't Heal*, New York, NY: Harmony Books, 1997.

Newton, Michael, Ph.D. *Destiny of Souls, New Case Studies of Life Between Lives*, St. Paul, MN: Llewellyn Publications, 2000.

————. *Journey of Souls*, St. Paul, MN: Llewellyn Publications, 2000.

Ovason, David. *The Secret Architecture of Our Nation's Capital*, New York, NY: Harper Collins, 1999, 2000.

Padel, Ruth. *I'm a Man, Sex, Gods and Rock 'n' Roll*, London, England: Faber and Faber Limited, 2000.

Padma, Ma Deva. *Tao Oracle,* New York, NY: St. Martin's Press, 2002.

Pollack, Rachel. *Seventy-Eight Degrees of Wisdom, A Book of Tarot,* Hammersmith, London: Thorsons, 1997.

Price, Catherine. *The Oglala People, 1841-1879: A Political History,* Lincoln, NE: University of Nebraska Press, 1996.

Radow Kliegman, Isabel. *Tarot and the Tree of Life,* Wheaton, IL: The Theosophical Publishing House, 1997.

Redfield, James and Carol Adrienne. *The Celestine Prophecy: An Experiential Guide,* New York, NY: Time Warner Co., 1995.

Rieder, Marge, Ph.D. *Mission to Millboro,* Nevada City, CA: Blue Dolphin Publishing, Inc., 1993.

———. *Return to Millboro,* Nevada City, CA: Blue Dolphin Publishing, Inc., 1996.

Rosetree, Rose. *The Power of Face Reading,* Sterling, VA: Women's Intuition Worldwide, 2001.

Ruiz, Don Miguel. *The Four Agreements,* San Rafael, CA: Amber-Allen, 1997.

Schneider, Michael S. *A Beginner's Guide to Constructing the Universe,* New York, NY: Harper Collins, 1994.

Semkiw, Walter, M.D. *Return of the Revolutionaries,* Charlottesville, VA: Hampton Roads, 2003.

Smedley, Jenny. *Ripples,* Norwich, England: Third Floor Productions, 1998.

Smoley, Richard and Jay Kinney. *Hidden Wisdom: A Guide to Western Inner Traditions,* New York, NY: Penguin Publishing, 1999.

Sutphen, Dick. *Earthly Purpose,* New York, NY: Pocket Books, 1990.

Talbot, Michael. *The Holographic Universe,* New York, NY: Harper Collins, 1991.

Tame, David. *The Secret Power of Music,* Rochester, VT: Destiny Books, 1984.

Tognetti, Arlene and Lisa Lenard. *The Complete Idiots Guide to Tarot and Fortune-Telling,* Indianapolis, IN: Alpha Books, 1999.

Tolle, Eckhart. *The Power of Now,* Novato, CA: New World Library, 1999.

———. *A New Earth,* New York, NY: Dutton, 2005.

Van Dyke, Deborah. *Travelling the Sacred Sound Current,* Bowen Island, B.C., Canada: Sound Current Music, 2001.

Walsch, Neale Donald. *The Little Soul and the Sun,* Charlottesville, VA: Hampton Roads, 1998.

———. *Conversations with God, Book 1,* New York, NY: Putnam Publishing Group, 1996.

———. *Conversations with God, Book 2,* Charlottesville, VA: Hampton Roads, 1997.

———. *Conversations with God, Book 3,* Charlottesville, VA: Hampton Roads, 1998.

Wambach, Helen, Ph.D. *Reliving Past Lives,* New York, NY: Barnes and Noble Books, 1974, 2000.

Weiss, Brian L., M.D. *Only Love is Real,* New York, NY: Time Warner, 1996.

Wolf, Fred Alan, Ph.D. *Matter into Feeling,* Portsmouth, NH: Moment Point Press, 2002.

————. *Mind into Matter,* Portsmouth, NH: Moment Point Press, 2000.

Zalkind Spear, Deena. *Ears of the Angels,* Carlsbad, CA: Hay House Inc., 2002.

Zukav, Gary. *The Dancing Wu Li Masters,* New York, NY: William-Morrow & Co., Inc., 1979.

ENDNOTES

The opinions shared on the websites cited as sources for some of the content of this book are not necessarily the opinions or viewpoints of the author or publisher.

[1] Jenny Boyd, Ph.D., *Musicians in Tune*, (New York, NY: Fireside, 1992), 184

[2] Michael C. Luckman, *Alien Rock*, (VH1/Pocket Books, 2005), 73. Quoted from William Blake, *The Marriage of Heaven and Hell*, 1793.

[3] *Ibid.* 73

[4] Spiritwalk, *Readings: On Waking Up*, Anthony DeMello, (http://www.geocities.com/~spiritwalk/demelloawake.htm), 2008

[5] Way of Life Literature, *Rock Musicians As Mediums*, (http://www.way-oflife.org/fbns/rockmusciansmediums.html) 2008. Quoted from *Down Beat*, June 1985, 61

[6] Fred Alan Wolf, *I Do Get Questions*, (http://www.fredalanwolf.com/page5.htm), 2008

[7] Ester and Jerry Hicks, *Ask and It Is Given*, (Hay House Inc., 2004), 48

[8] Brainy Quotes, *Eric Clapton* (http://www.brainyquote.com/quotes/quotes/e/ericclapto264638.html), 2008

[9] Ted Andrews, *Dream Alchemy: Shaping our Dreams To Transform Our Lives*, (Llewellyn Publications, 1991), 15

[10] Susie and Otto's Love and Relationships article, *Soul Mates and Twin Flames* by Ariana Masters, (http://www.soulmaterelationships.com/soul-matearticles/soulmatedefinition.htm), 2008

[11] Michael Newton, Ph.D., *Destiny of Souls, New Case Studies of Life Between Lives*, (Llewellyn Publications, 2000), 275

[12] Spirit Portal, *Merlin's Magical Mystery School-Spiritual Healing*, (http://www.spiritportal.org/soul.html), 2008

[13] P.M.H. Atwater, *Future Memory: How those who 'See the Future' shed new light on the workings of the human mind*, (http://www.cinemind.com/atwater/future.html), 2008

[14] Way of Life Literature, *Rock Musicians as Mediums*, (http://www.way-oflife.org/fbns/rockmusciansmediums.html), 2008. Quoted from *Circus*, January, 31, 1984, 70

[15] Deepak Chopra, *Spontaneous Fulfillment of Desire*, (Harmony Books, 2003), 237–238

[16] Stenudd.com, *Psychoanalysis of Myth*, (http://www.stenudd.com/myth/freudjung/jung-archetypes.htm), 2008

[17] Deborah Van Dyke, *Travelling the Sacred Sound Current*, (Sound Current Music, 2001), 31, quoted from *The Music of Life*, by Hazrat Inayat Khan

[18] Brainy Quotes, *Bonnie Raitt Quotes*, (http://www.brainyquote.com/quotes/authors/b/bonnie_raitt.html), 2008

[19] Jenny Smedley, (http://www.users.globalnet.co.uk/~author/about.htm), 2008

[20] Dick Sutphen, *Earthly Purpose*, (Pocketbooks, 1990), Introduction, ix

[21] Masaru Emoto, *The Hidden Messages in Water*, (Beyond Words Publishing, 2004), 116

[22] Jonathan Goldman, *Healing Sounds*, (Healing Arts Press, 2002), 18

[23] Mary Montano, *Loving Mozart*, (Cantus Verus Books, 1995), 115

[24] Deborah Van Dyke, *Travelling the Sacred Sound Current*, (Sound Current Music, 2001), 46, quoted from *Toning – The Creative Power of the Voice* by Laurel Elizabeth Keyes

[25] Jonathan Goldman, *Healing Sounds*, (Healing Arts Press, 2002), 87

[26] *Ibid.* 20–21

[27] *Ibid.* 22

[28] Mickey Hart, *Spirit into Sound: The Magic of Music*, (Grateful Dead Productions and Acid Test Productions, 1999), 33

[29] Jonathan Goldman, *Healing Sounds*, (Healing Arts Press, 2002), 11

[30] Richard Smoley, *Hidden Wisdom: A Guide to Western Inner Traditions*, (Penguin Publishing, 1999), 108. Quoted from *The Black Arts*, by Richard Cavendish.

[31] Mickey Hart, *Spirit into Sound: The Magic of Music*, (Grateful Dead Productions and Acid Test Productions, 1999), 98

[32] Jenny Boyd, Ph.D., *Musicians in Tune*, (New York, NY: Fireside, 1992), 54

[33] Dr. Duck, *Music Quotes, Advice & Famous Last Words*, (http://www.ducksdeluxe.com/quotes.html), 2008

[34] Jenny Boyd, Ph.D., *Musicians in Tune*, (Fireside, 1992), 86

[35] Gaia Community, *Science of Mind Interviews, 2002 and 2006 – Eckhart Tolle*, (http://drs1958.gaia.com/blog/2008/3/science_of_mind_interviews_2002_and_2006_eckhart_tolle), 2008

[36] Mickey Hart, *Spirit into Sound,* (Grateful Dead Productions and Acid Test Productions, 1999), 148

[37] Vibrani's One Source, *The Oversoul,* (http://www.vibrani.com/oversoul.htm), 2008

[38] Mike Hayes and Ken Sharp, *Reputation is a Fragile Thing,* (Poptastic!, 1998), Foreword

[39] Better Living-Living Life to the Max, *Are You A Lightworker?* (http://www.betterliving.co.nz/content/theFamily/new-age/Are-You-A-Lightworker.aspx), 2008

[40] DecozNumerology, *Do Your Own Numerology Reading, Your LifePath is 11,* (http://www.decoz.com/Numerology_LifePath_D.htm), 2008

[41] QuoteWorld.org, *QuoteWorld, Life, Maurice Druon,* (http://www.quote-world.org/category/life/author/maurice_druon), 2008

[42] Claudia Wallis and Kristina Dell, "What Makes Teens Tick," *Time,* May 10, 2004

[43] Healing Sounds, *Sonic Entrainment,* (http://www.healingsounds.com/articles/sonic-entrainment.asp), 2008

[44] Mickey Hart, *Drumming at the Edge of Magic,* (Harper Collins, 1990), 112

[45] Timothy White, *Rock Lives,* (Henry Holt and Company, 1990), 592

[46] Mike Hayes and Ken Sharp, *Reputation is a Fragile Thing,* (Poptastic!, 1998), 140

[47] David Tame, *The Secret Power of Music,* (Destiny Books, 1984), 190

[48] *Ibid.* 135

[49] Connection Magazine, *Quotes on Music, Sound, and Silence,* (http://members.chello.nl/whessel/connection/quote_e.htm), 2008

[50] Michael Schneider, *A Beginner's Guide to Constructing the Universe,* (Harper Collins, 1994), 292–293

[51] Gaia Community, *A Quote by Albert Camus,* (http://www.gaia.com/quotes/906/truly_fertile_music_the_only/by_albert_camus?), 2008

[52] Catherine Price, *The Oglala People, 1841–1879: A Political History,* (University of Nebraska Press, 1996), preface x

[53] Jenny Boyd, Ph.D., *Musicians in Tune,* (New York, NY: Fireside, 1992), 139

[53a] Mike Hayes and Ken Sharp, *Reputation is a Fragile Thing,* (Poptastic!, 1998), 140

[54] Wikipedia, *Rosicrucians,* (http://en.wikipedia.org/wiki/Rosicrucian), 2008

[55] BibliOdyssey, *The Temple of Music,* (http://bibliodyssey.blogspot.com/2007/02/temple-of-music.html), 2008

[56] Alchemy Wesbsite, *Doctor Robert Fludd (1574–1637),* (http://www.alchemywebsite.com/fludd1.html), 2008

[57] J.B. Craven, *Dr. Robert Fludd: The English Rosicrucian,* (Kessinger Publishing; Facsimiled edition, 1992), 72

[58] Order of the Grail, *The"(Al)Chemical Wedding" of Christian Rosenkreutz, and the Archetypal Sevenfold Pattern of Transformation,* www.orderofthe-grail.org/chemical_wedding_of_crc.htm), 2008

[59] Joceyln Goodwin, *Robert Fludd,* (Phanes Press, 1991), 6

[60] Jenny Boyd, Ph.D., *Musicians in Tune,* (Fireside, 1992), 115

[61] Rachel Pollack, *Seventy-Eight Degrees of Wisdom, A Book of Tarot,* (Thorsons, 1997), 155–156

[62] Greg Braden, *The God Code,* (Hay House, 2004), 140

[63] Behnke Technologies, Music Quotes.txt, (http://www.behnketech.com/MusicQuotes.txt), 2008

[64] Theosophy Library Online, (www.theosophy.org), article cited 2004, (no longer found, 2008)

[65] Wikipedia, *Great White Brotherhood,* (http://en.wikipedia.org/wiki/Great_White_Brotherhood), 2008

[66] William James, *The Varieties of Religious Experience,* (http://www.csp.org/experience/james-varieties/james-varieties16.html), 2008

[67] Graveworm, *The Swastika,* (http://www.graveworm.com/occult/sacred/swa.html), 2008

[68] Wikipedia, *Archangel Michael,* (http://en.wikipedia.org/wiki/Michael_(archangel), 2008

[69] Brainyquote, *Jimi Hendix Quotes,* (http://www.brainyquote.com/quotes/quotes/j/jimihendri294547.html), 2008

[70] Ma Deva Padma, *The Tao Oracle* deck and book, (St. Martins Press, 2002), 124

[71] Brainyquote, *Billy Joel* (http://www.brainyquote.com/quotes/quotes/b/billyjoel133275.html), 2008

[72] Wikipedia, *Karma,* (http://en.wikipedia.org/wiki/Karma), 2008

[73] Deepak Chopra, *The Seven Spiritual Laws of Success*, (Amber-Allen & New World Library, 1994), 46

[74] *Ibid.* 46

[75] *Ibid.* 98

[76] Deborah Van Dyke, *Travelling the Sacred Sound Current*, (Sound Current Music, 2001), 143

[77] *Ibid.* 147

[78] A Way of Life Literature, *Rock Music as Religion*, (http://www.wayoflife.org/fbns/rockmusic-religion.html), 2008. Quoted from *"Why Knock Rock?* by Dan and Steve Peters.

[79] Timothy Freke and Peter Gandy, *Jesus and the Lost Goddess*, (Crown Publishing, 2002), 160

[80] Hulu Project, *Shamanism and Music*, (http://www.hulu.de/shamanism/shamanism.htm), 2008

[81] The Well, *Introduction to an Eleusinian Revival*, Donald P. Dulchinos (http://www.well.com/user/dpd/shaman.html), 2008. Quoted from *Hallucinogens: Cross Cultural Perspectives* by Marlene Dobkin de Rios.

[82] Limelight Agency, *Experience Kruger's Hendrix*, (http://www.limelightagency.com/Sebastian_Kruger/anounse/hendrix/Hendrix_public.html), 2008

[83] Jenny Boyd, Ph.D., *Musicians in Tune*, (New York, NY: Fireside, 1992), 131

[84] Famous Quotes, *U2*, (http://www.musicwithease.com/u2-quotes.html), 2008

[85] Return of the Revolutionaries: Evidence of Reincarnation, *Nexus* , May/June 2004, back cover

[86] Walter Semkiw, MD, *Return of the Revolutionaries*, (Hampton Roads, 2003), 36

[87] *Ibid.* 37

[88] Deborah Van Dyke, *Travelling the Sacred Sound Current*, (Sound Current Music, 2001), 153. Quoted from *The Secret Music of the Soul* by Patrick Bernhardt.

[89] Deborah Van Dyke, *Travelling the Sacred Sound Current*, (Sound Current Music, 2001), 154. Quoted from *The Creative Sound* by Torkom Saraydarian.

APPENDIX

The following images are from the Universal Waite Tarot deck ©US Games. For more information on the Tarot, check out Joan Bunning's website, http://www.learntarot.com or her book, *Learning the Tarot: A Tarot Book for Beginners.*

The Fool

The Magician

The Emporer

Judgement

The Tower

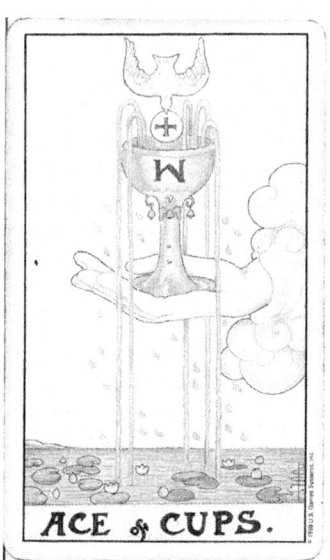

Ace of Cups

Page of Swords

Three of Wands

Ten of Pentacles

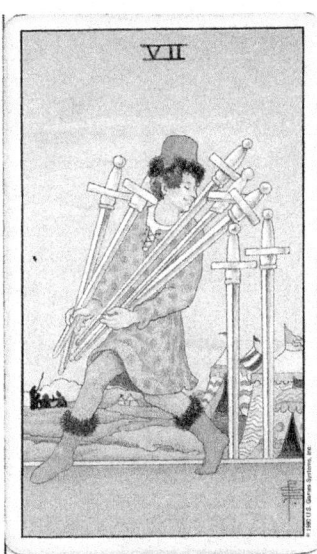

Seven of Swords

Five of Pentacles

Eight of Cups

Robert Fludd's Temple of Music

INDEX

A NOTE TO READERS

Wanna know more about reincarnation, intuitives, the books I've read, my rock music survey, blog, and other cool stuff? Check out my website www.soundofyoursoul.com. You'll find:

- Deleted Scenes: I've got a ton of material that ended up on the editing floor. If you want to delve a bit deeper into quantum physics, reincarnation, the divine feminine, my wacky dreams, numerology, the Tarot, transcriptions of several intuitive readings and more, check out this page.

- Intuitives: For brief bios of the psychics I consulted and their contact info, visit the "My Links" page.

- Bibliography: For an online compilation of the books mentioned, go to the "Bibliography" page, and click the "my library" link.

- Book trailer: Can you find the hidden clues?

- Glossary: Lots of cool info, with links to related websites.

If the Tarot piqued your interest, a complete list of the Universal Waite Tarot cards, with images and descriptions, can be found at Joan Bunning's website www.learntarot.com.

Are you a member of a spiritual group or book club? Would you like to chat? I'd be delighted to speak with your group by teleconference. You can also order discounted group quantities of this book at my website.

Have you had a mystical or spiritual experience with music? Drop me a line. I'd love to hear from you.

Warmest regards,

Laura Faeth

laura@soundofyoursoul.com

www.myspace.com/talltrickster

CPSIA information can be obtained
at www.ICGtesting.com
Printed in the USA
BVOW06s0838141116

467771BV00021B/226/P